# HE IS OUR PEACE

# He is our
# Peace

## Meditations on
## Christian Nonviolence

*From the writings of
Howard Goeringer, Eberhard Arnold,
Christoph F. Blumhardt, and others*

Edited by Emmy Barth

© 1994 Plough Publishing House
The Hutterian Brethren Service Committee

Farmington PA 15437, USA
Robertsbridge, East Sussex TN32 5DR, England

Library of Congress Cataloging-in-publication data

He is our peace: meditations on Christian nonviolence: from the
  writings of Howard Goeringer, Eberhard Arnold,
  J. Heinrich Arnold, Christoph F. Blumhardt, and others/
  edited by Emmy Barth.
      p. cm.
    Includes bibliographical references.
    ISBN: 0-87486-064-4
    1. Nonviolence–Religious aspects–Christianity. 2. Peace–
Religious aspects–Christianity.    I Barth, Emmy, 1961-
BT736.6.H4  1994                                      94-6086
261.8'73–dc20                                              CIP

Printed in the USA

# CONTENTS

# PREFACE

FOR MANY YEARS Howard Goeringer has witnessed
to Christ and his reconciling love. He has ministered to the
poor and the oppressed, drug addicts, and under-privi-
leged minorities. For the past ten years he has shared his
convictions with a wider audience through his newsletter,
*The Jesus Journal.*

Howard searched long for a church that held to the
faith and practices of the earliest Christians. He knew from
his studies that for the first years following Christ's resurrection Christianity was alive with God's Spirit. The believers were of one heart and soul, filled with joy, breaking
bread together, and sharing their possessions (Acts 2:46–
47, 4:32). They refused to take part in any violence, for
they were filled with love for one another and for all men.
Howard wondered, "Was there still such a church today?"

In 1986 Howard came into contact with the Hutterian
Brethren, an Anabaptist group dating to the 1530s. The
Anabaptists protested not only the corruption of the
Catholic Church but also the limitations of the Protestant
Reformation. In their eyes, Christ demanded a more
radical discipleship: the baptism not of infants but of adult
believers, the refusal to bear arms, chastity before marriage
and faithfulness within it, and brotherly community.

Violent persecution followed the founding of the first Anabaptist congregation in Zürich in 1525. Especially hard hit were the Hutterites, a branch of the Anabaptists who were perhaps more visible than others because of their settlement in communal villages or "Bruderhofs" throughout Moravia and Slovakia. Like other Anabaptists, the Hutterites did not resist, but suffered patiently as Christ commanded: "Do not resist one who is evil" (Mt. 5:39).

As the Hutterite movement spread, persecution by state and ecclesiastical authorities increased, and the group fled: to east-central Europe in the 18th Century, to Russia in the 19th, and to North America in the 1870s. Throughout this odyssey the Hutterites held unswervingly to their belief in nonviolence. World War I saw the death of two Hutterite men imprisoned for their refusal to bear arms, and in World War II, the Korean War, and the Vietnam War, hundreds of Hutterites performed alternative service as conscientious objectors.

After retiring from his work as editor of *The Jesus Journal,* Howard Goeringer turned to the Hutterian Bruderhofs with a request: Would we help him publish a selection of his writings, combining our voices with his in one witness to Jesus' call for peace? This book is the result of Howard's request.

*Emmy Barth*

# INTRODUCTION

I HAVE BEEN ASKED to explain how I came to my commitment to nonviolence and my rejection of the military and its politics. This is my answer.

I was baptized and confirmed in St. Luke's Reformed Church in Wilkes-Barre, Pennsylvania. Ulrich Zwingli, recognized as the sixteenth century founding father of the Reformed Church in Switzerland, was killed on a battlefield killing Catholics. So the church that baptized and nurtured me in the faith is obviously not one of the historic "peace churches." Two of my four brothers served in the military and, along with my father, were very much involved in American politics—which is inseparable from violence. All in all, mine was a typical family in a typical mainline church that accepted violence and the war system just as they accepted the rising and setting of the sun each day.

In looking back, I recognize that in my youth I idolized sports; my life was centered on the ambition to make the varsity team in the three major sports.

On a January day while shooting baskets in the church gym, I noticed a few red blotches on my body. Chicken pox. I notified the coach I would be out for a couple of weeks.

Not only did I not return to the team—I did not return to school for the rest of the term. With no ball to shoot or dribble, no brothers or sisters at home to talk to, and fifty-year-old parents I loved, but never really felt close to as far as intimate sharing of problems, I was confronted for the first time with a reality I was not able to cope with: death and the fact that the athletic body my life centered on would turn to dust.

At the age of sixteen I experienced "the dark night of the soul." Fully conscious of the transitory nature of my life, I searched the scriptures for an answer. I found myself questioning the different churches and what they stood for.

My brother had a large tract of land in the Poconos where I spent time working, camping, hunting, fishing, and enjoying the healing of God's nature and out-of-doors. I thought of myself as a Christian. I had a lot of information about Jesus and the church. Still, there was uncertainty, dark fears, a sense of aloneness. No deep joy in living. No peace of soul.

Asking, seeking, knocking, I prayed for an answer, for certainty. Without warning, the answer was given. Light dispelled my soul's darkness, and the demon of fear was cast out.

It was spring. The sun was just above the horizon. My cousin and I were sitting in the back of the farm pickup truck with fishing tackle and bait, ready for a couple of hours on a favorite trout stream.

As we turned out of the drive onto the highway, the heavens opened. The evening sky was filled with a great throng of people in fellowship. In that moment of vision I was overcome with joy and an awareness of God's presence that is as real to me now as it was then, more than sixty years ago. In that God-event I experienced the peace of Jesus that prevails in his kingdom—a peace that is not a hope to be achieved through political and military power before the day of Christ comes, nor a gift that must wait for the end time to be opened and enjoyed. It is the present climate that prevails in the present kingdom into which Jesus brings us via his saving acts.

I do not call myself a pacifist. There are a hundred different kinds of pacifism. I am a disciple of Jesus, of whom the prophet said, "A bruised reed he will not break" (Is. 42:3).

Nor do I think of myself as a conscientious objector. My commitment to nonviolence does not depend upon my conscience at any given moment. It depends on this: I am a disciple of Jesus who said, "Take up your cross and follow me" (Mt. 16:24). The love Jesus demonstrated on the cross does not inflict suffering; it absorbs suffering for the sake of a world redeemed.

Jesus' teaching could not be clearer: "A new commandment I give to you, that you love one another; even as I have loved you" (Jn. 13:34). "Love your enemies and pray for those who persecute you" (Mt. 5:44). "Peace I leave with you; my peace I give to you; not as the world gives do I give to you" (Jn. 14:27).

Reconciliation is a way of life, the way of the cross. It applies to all of my life. Jesus, my one Lord, is not a split personality. My experience of God brought a new wholeness into my life, the wholeness of holiness in Christ. Nonviolence, peace, and wholeness are synonyms.

On a mountaintop I experienced the reality of God in Jesus. I have come to know him as a person and as gospel truth. His gospel is clear. As a Christian my only option is to obey his word, day by day, in all the decisions I make.

*H. Goeringer*

# CHRISTIAN NONVIOLENCE

*"Then the peace of God, which is beyond our utmost understanding, will keep guard over your hearts and your thoughts, in Christ Jesus"* (Phil. 4:7).

O LORD GOD, grant us your Spirit, that we may comprehend your peace. As we pray, help us to recognize what must come from you alone, for you are mighty and holy and your will is peace on earth. Your will is peace beyond all understanding, your peace in heaven and on earth and under the earth, your peace that opposes all sin and death and takes away every evil that can be named. We await you, O Lord our God, and you will hear us. No matter how long the battle lasts, we will hold out in patience, for we are your children. We shall never lose the faith that your name shall be honored and that all things shall come into harmony with your will of peace on earth, your peace. Amen.

*C. F. Blumhardt* [1]

2 JESUS' TEACHING concerning the way to respond to evil could not be clearer: "You have heard that it was said, 'An eye for an eye and a tooth for a tooth.' But I say to you, Do not resist one who is evil. But if anyone strikes you on the right cheek, turn to him the other also. You have heard that it was said, 'You shall love your neighbor and hate your enemy.' But I say to you, Love your enemies and pray for those who persecute you, so that you may be sons of your Father who is in heaven (Mt. 5:38–39, 43–45).

This teaching of nonviolence was clear to Paul, and he taught it to the Church at Rome (Rom. 12:14–21). Jesus' teaching of nonviolence was clear to Peter as we read in his letter to the Church in Asia (1 Pt. 2:23). Jesus' teaching of nonviolence was clear to all the leaders in the early church as we hear Origen echo their unanimous message to the world: "No longer do we take the sword against any nation, nor do we learn war any more, since we have become sons of peace through Jesus who is our author instead of following the traditional customs, by which we were strangers to the covenants" (Contra Celsum, v. 33).

*H. Goeringer*

LIFE IS GROWTH and development. Life is the    3
unfolding of love. Killing does not belong to life. It belongs
to death. Thus violence and coercion do not belong to
growth but to the stifling of life. We have been entrusted
with witnessing to only that which serves life and builds
life. It makes no difference whether the growth of this life
appears to be evolutionary or revolutionary. It means both
development and upheaval at the same time, because it
means casting off that which wants to die. Life means to
give and bestow what awakens life. Yet no evolution, no
upheaval is able to eradicate the deepest root of all world
suffering: universal guilt, the lethal poison of evil, of hate,
covetous lust, depravity, and killing.

*E. Arnold* [2]

*4*  IF YOU FEEL URGED to try to prevent or postpone a
war, we can only rejoice. But what troubles us is whether
you will have much success in opposing the war spirit that
exists right now:

When in China and Russia millions of people starve to
death while in Argentina and other countries millions of
tons of wheat are stockpiled, isn't that war?

When thousands of women prostitute their bodies and
their lives are ruined for the sake of money, isn't that war?

When each year millions of babies are murdered by
abortion, isn't that war?

When people are forced to work like slaves because they
can hardly provide the milk and bread for their children,
isn't that war?

When the wealthy live in villas surrounded by parks while
in other districts there are families who don't even have a
room to themselves, isn't that war?

When one person assumes the right to build up a huge
bank account while another can scarcely earn enough for
basic necessities, isn't that war?

When automobiles, driven at a speed agreeable to the
owners, kill sixty thousand people a year in the United
States, isn't that war?

*E. Arnold* [3]

CHRISTIAN NONVIOLENCE is not achieved by              5
peace movements protesting the nuclear arms race—
although Christians must protest such destructive use of
God's gift of the world's resources. The invention of
nuclear weapons did not suddenly change the nature of
evil, only its increased capacity to kill and destroy. Jesus is
not primarily a "No" to the weapons of violence. Jesus is
God's "Yes" to the New Creation of agape whose only
weapon is the sword of the Spirit. It is to bear witness to
this kingdom of agape that the Church is sent.

*H. Goeringer*

CHRISTIAN NONVIOLENCE is not a hope for peace
in the future, achieved only by the second coming of
Christ. The good news of the gospel is all about something
God has already done in Jesus' first coming, calling for the
complete yielding of our will to his Holy Spirit now.

*H. Goeringer*

6  THE REASON I don't like the word "pacifist" is because Jesus teaches us to fight—with his kind of weapons. An old Georgia farmer said to Clarence Jordan, founder of Koinonia Farm, "I heard you won't fight."

"Who told you that?" Clarence replied. "We sure will fight."

Surprised, the farmer said, "Well, you won't go into the army, will you?"

"No, we don't fight that way," said Clarence. "Do you see that mule over there? Now, if that mule bit you, would you bite it back?"

"Nope," replied the farmer. "I'd hit that mule with a two-by-four and knock its head off."

"Exactly," replied Clarence. "You wouldn't let the mule set the level of your encounter with him. You would get a weapon a mule doesn't know how to handle, but you do. Well, that's what Christians are supposed to do—use weapons of the Spirit Jesus uses, not weapons of the world the enemy uses."

*H. Goeringer*

CHRISTIAN NONVIOLENCE is not a political action     7
strategy to try to achieve peace on earth by getting Christian leaders into government and hoping their voting
record will make the United States  a "Christian" nation.
There never was a "Christian" state, and there never will
be. Every state lives by an ethic of survival and uses force to
survive, force that is willing to do anything to protect
national interests. In sharp contrast is the way of the cross
that teaches us to lose our life loving and serving the world
just as Jesus did. This is foolishness to the state, which
cannot possibly live by the creed of the apostles who
shouted in victory, "The third day he rose from the dead."
Christians do not need the survival kit offered by the
Pentagon. Our assurance of survival is the resurrection life
we share in the kingdom God inaugurated on Good
Friday's cross and Easter's empty tomb—he is risen!

*H. Goeringer*

*8*   WE HAVE ALWAYS fought against a purely utilitarian pacifism, because this pacifism proved to be a failure in practical life. I got to know people, for instance, who spoke in meetings of pacifist circles against hatred and against war, but who were unable to live peacefully with their own wives. And this brings us to the root of the matter.

Nowhere do we find Jesus saying a single word to support a theoretical, utilitarian pacifism. But Jesus did show us the deepest reason for us to live in total nonviolence and to never injure or harm our fellow beings in body or soul. Where does this deep inner direction of Jesus Christ come from? There are some who misunderstand Jesus utterly and think there was a kind of feminine softness in him. His own words prove that this is not true. He says that his way will lead us into the hardest battle and bring us not only into the most desperate inner situations but even to physical death. His own death and his whole attitude, the sureness and fearlessness with which he met the powers of murder and untruthfulness, prove this.

*E. Arnold* [4]

THE WORD "PACIFIST" does not belong in the      9
vocabulary of the Christian. Pacifism implies the refusal to
fight and engage in war. For Christians there must also be
the cross—the giving of self to God for the sake of others.
And there must be the resurrection that follows the cross,
the absolute certainty that we have protection in the Christ,
who comes to us with the good news that he has overcome
the evil and death of our fallen world and offers us victory.

*H. Goeringer*

*10*   GANDHI'S USE of nonviolence as a weapon of defense
has significance for the whole world today. There is no
doubt that Gandhi was influenced in a decisive way both by
currents of ancient Indian religion and by the practical way
of life which Christ outlined in his Sermon on the Mount.
But in hours of quiet and reflection Gandhi clung not to
the New Testament nor to the Sermon on the Mount but
to the ancient Indian scriptures. Gandhi reposed faith in
his Indian people, a faith much greater than anything
Christ said in his day about the people of Israel. In Gandhi
nonviolence, that loving activity of passive resistance, is
subsidiary to the achieving of success, success for the
people of India. There is no denying that Gandhi was
influenced by current politics.

With Christ it was quite different. His way is the nonviolence which leads to taking full sacrifice upon oneself as
the task of one's life. His faith is not trusting in the immor-
tality of a man or a people. His faith is rather believing in
such a resurrection that the man who is arisen lives quite
differently from his former life. The only attitude towards
the present world which is valid in Jesus is the recognition
that over all division and sin hangs death. But this recognition also means faith in resurrection and in the new
creation which comes from God alone. The only faith
which Jesus has is faith in God. So long as we keep this
essential distinction clear before our eyes, we can learn

immeasurably from Gandhi, for he had the courage to put 11
his inner convictions into practice in his public life amid
the realities of racial and social problems.

*E. Arnold* [5]

*12* CHRISTIAN NONVIOLENCE is not a human achievement, certainly not a possibility of state. It is the life of the spirit that comes to us from God. It means simply loving one another as Jesus on the cross loved us. Jesus' love for us was not a human achievement in the sense that he based his life on a self-contained ethic that called for nonviolence. Jesus is the self revelation of God—God revealing his unconditional and holy love to us.

It is essential that Christians understand this inseparable link between God's living Spirit and nonviolence. Without this understanding two things result: one, nonviolence is regarded as something separate from the gospel that we can take or leave; two, it becomes a method of problem solving based on our own human values. Both are wrong. For the Christian nonviolence is not an option, it is the only way—the way of the cross that becomes possible when we completely abandon our life to the risen Lord and freely choose to let his love control our lives.

*H. Goeringer*

We are conscientious objectors to war.     *13*
We are asked, "What is the point of declaring that we will
not bear arms when faced with grave danger?" The answer
is simple: if I have come to such a recognition—that I
cannot bear arms—then it is impossible for me to act
otherwise in my personal life. Schiller answers this in
another way in his drama *The Thirty Years' War:* he writes
that there is no danger that will actually force a man to
murder, and that no war is really waged for the sake of
ideals—it is always a matter of material interests.

If love is not practiced in one's own small circle, pacifism becomes a mere phrase. Peace must be tested in daily
life. A sort of general pacifism does not interest us—only a
pacifism which permeates the whole of life through the
Good Spirit.

Pacifism arises from inner conversion, and that is what is
decisive. There are people who have no conception of
Christ and yet are pacifists. The important thing is whether
the spirit in them is one of "Love your enemies." This does
not mean merely accepting them, but embracing them
with love in action. Christ's strength is often unconsciously
present. Whatever takes place, takes place through him.
When someone is driven by love in any way, he is driven by
Christ. Whoever has love, has the love of God, even if he
does not confess Christ in words. There is a hidden Christ;
he is much too great to be confined to a little circle. He is a
person and not a concept.

*E. Arnold* [6]

*14*  WHAT IS CALLED the peace movement muddies the water of nonviolence by trying to pressure governments to practice nonviolence as a policy. Many within the church limit peace-making to the kind of political effort that makes of nonviolence a separate policy that can be attached to government like a tail on a kite. But Christian nonviolence is the kite that can fly only in the atmosphere of the deathless spirit revealed on the cross and at the resurrection.

For the Christian, nonviolence can only be understood within the context of God's mighty acts of salvation in the person of Jesus and his proclamation of the kingdom of God within our history. These were his first words that summarized what his gospel is all about: "The time is fulfilled, and the kingdom of God is at hand; repent, and believe in the gospel." In this gospel is salvation that releases those who want to become citizens of God's kingdom from the curse of violence and war and their tragic consequences: evil and death.

*H. Goeringer*

THE COMMON IDEA of peace is the absence of war    *15*
between nations. The corollary to this is that such peace is
achieved by international diplomacy and, when this fails,
by military action and victory on the battlefield. For
centuries the church has accepted this definition of
collective peace, separating it from Jesus' Sermon on the
Mount. To achieve this peace, the church says it is necessary at times to engage in violent wars. Since Jesus spoke of
rumors of war until the close of the age, we must have
military power to prepare for war.

Alongside this concept of collective peace, the church
preaches a more intimate and personal peace to which
forgiveness and the love of enemies is supposed to apply.
Thus we hear the church teaching Christian youth to
refrain from person-to-person violence, but to join the
armed forces to learn mass violence and killing to protect
that nation from enemies.

*H. Goeringer*

*16*   SOME WANT TO TALK exclusively about the peace of
their own soul or the peace they share with another. They
are incapable of representing the whole peace of God that
belongs to the final Kingdom. They remain sunk in
narrow-minded folly, bogged down in the swamp of
isolation. But it is the same with those friends of peace
who make the opposite mistake and speak about world
peace without peace with God and without the social
justice of complete community. They want "pacifism"
without fighting the spirits of unpeace, without battling
the covetous nature of mammon, without opposing the
accepted lies of social insincerity, and without waging
spiritual warfare against unfaithfulness and impurity. Both
of these false paths in life represent unpeace that comes
from folly and indifference to all-embracing truth.

*E. Arnold* [7]

THE GOSPEL OF PEACE is demonstrated on the     *17*
cross where God's agape love in Jesus overcomes the
world's worst evil with good. In his resurrection Jesus gives
his church the victory of peace that no other power can
give—victory over sin's death whenever we choose to
repent and live here and now in the peace of agape love.
In Jesus' Holy Spirit of love we receive the power to witness
to the reality of the peace that this world can neither give
nor take from us. Such is the good news of peace we
proclaim when we put on the whole armor of God. Jesus
did not ask the political kingdom of Rome to build peace.
He does not ask the political kingdom of the United States
to achieve this peace. What Jesus does ask is that his
church proclaim and practice the gospel of peace he has
already achieved. We either have God's peace in Jesus, or
we have nothing.

*H. Goeringer*

*18*   WHAT WE CALL Christian nonviolence is nothing
more nor less than agape—the new life in Christ that God
gives to the meek, the poor in spirit, those who hunger and
thirst for righteousness, and those who mourn for their
sins and, turning from the world, surrender their life to
God's holy will in Christ. The abandonment of violence
for protection and as the way to achieve a goal makes
absolutely no sense apart from agape. Agape is God's gift
of the Holy Spirit in the crucified and risen Lord of life.
Retaliation and violent killing is the way sin functions in
our fallen world. Reconciliation and nonviolent forgiveness and mercy is the way agape lives in the kingdom of
God. Agape is the first fruit of that kingdom.

*H. Goeringer*

THE CHRISTIAN PEACE WITNESS is to love as          *19*
Jesus loved and to walk moment by moment in the way of
his nonviolent cross. Christian nonviolence is living in
Christ and his kingdom of agape. Nothing more. Nothing
less. The Christian protest is not against nuclear war and
certain types and numbers of weapons. It is against all war
and all weapons and the military system itself. For Christians the so-called nuclear freeze is a farce—or should be.
It is the system and the spirit of violence that agape
opposes, not the type and the number of weapons.

*H. Goeringer*

20  SOME PEOPLE may see their task in the upholding of
law and order by murderous means; others may believe
they are called to fight for the proletariat, for a future of
justice and peace with bloodstained fists; others may regard
their own race as a holy shrine and declare war on another
race. Our life is filled with a content which has deeper
roots. A life task has been entrusted to us which looks
further ahead. The mystery of life has been revealed to us.
It has dawned upon us because Christ means everything to
us. We feel united with the whole church of Christ, in
which no group or individual can live in isolation from the
rest. Both the one and the other are members and organs
of the one living body, the Spirit, head, and heart of which
is the coming Christ. Hence the testimony of our life is
nothing but the essence of Christ's own life. He discloses
the mystery of life to us when he points to the birds in the
air at springtime, to the flowers in the meadow, when he
expects good fruits only from the healthy tree, when he
reveals the heart of the Father to us, the Father who sends
his rain and his sunshine on both the good and the bad.

*E. Arnold* [8]

WE BELIEVE in the new birth of a life of light from      *21*
God. We believe in the future of love and in the construc-
tive fellowship of men. We believe in the peace of God's
kingdom, and we believe that he will come to this earth.
This faith is not a playing with a future shape of things
which exists only in our imagination now. No. The same
God who will bring this future gives us his heart and his
spirit today. His name is the *I Am Who I Am.* His nature is
the same now as it will reveal itself in the future. He
revealed his heart in Jesus. He gives us his Spirit in Christ's
presence among us. In his church, the embodiment of
Christ's life, he lives the life of Jesus once again. This
church is the hidden living seed of the future Kingdom.
The character of peace and the love-spirit of the future
have been entrusted to her. Therefore she practices justice
and peace and joy in this world, also in the present age.

*E. Arnold* [9]

# PEACE IN THE OLD TESTAMENT

**ALMIGHTY GOD,** stretch out your hand over the    *23*
whole world. Let your Spirit bring a new age, an age of
truth, righteousness, and love, an age of peace that comes
from you. O Lord God, we are your children, and as your
children we pray to you in the name of Jesus Christ. You
will hear us, and we look forward with joy to the time when
all promises will be fulfilled, the time spoken about by the
prophets, and especially by your Son, Jesus Christ. Be with
us and gather us in your Spirit. Amen.

*C. F. Blumhardt* [1]

*24* ISRAEL WAS GIVEN the vision and promise of
shalom. At times the vision faded and the promise was
forgotten as century followed century from Abraham to
Moses, to David, to Nehemiah. But there were always the
Jeremiahs to remind Israel of God's promised shalom:

> I will fulfill to you my promise and bring you back to this
> place. For I know the plans I have for you, says the Lord,
> plans for shalom, and not for evil, to give you a future
> and a hope (Jer. 29:10–11).

Old Testament visions of shalom finally became New
Testament reality of shalom in the God-Person who could
say what no other lips have ever dared to say: "Shalom I
leave with you; my shalom I give to you; not as the world
gives peace do I give to you" (Jn. 14:27).

*H. Goeringer*

THE HEBREW WORD for peace is "shalom." Shalom  25
is the substance of the biblical vision of one community
embracing all creation. Shalom implies well-being and the
wholeness of all life—material, spiritual, physical, personal,
corporate. Shalom is the reality of Paradise. Shalom is
eternal life in the holy caring and sharing community of
God's Spirit, the blessing promised to Abraham for the
salvation of all the families of the earth.

God created us for shalom—he created us to abide in
harmony with his Spirit and all creation for eternity. But
shalom cannot be forced upon us against our will. Shalom
is a gift freely given that must be freely received.

*H. Goeringer*

26    *"Seek the shalom of the city where I have sent you into exile, and pray to the Lord on its behalf, for in its shalom you will find your shalom"* (Jer. 29:7).

IN 600 BC the Babylonian army invaded Judah and took hostages from Jerusalem into exile. It was in these difficult circumstances that Jeremiah wrote these remarkable words to refugees in hated Babylon, where they were forced to live as exiles while they watched their Jewish culture collapse. Despising their captors, yearning to return to their homeland, and resenting God's failure to save them, they couldn't believe what Jeremiah was saying. This crazy man of God was telling them to love their captors, to do good to their enemies, to ask the Lord to bless their persecutors with shalom.

As we might expect, Jeremiah's letter was not popular, not a bestseller. The suffering hostages could not see how their well-being and the well-being of their captors were inseparably bound together. To think of serving their captors in a spirit of kindness, nursing their sick, teaching Babylonian children Jewish games, working an extra hour—this was utter foolishness.

*H. Goeringer*

WITH SO MUCH VIOLENCE in it, how can the Old 27
Testament be part of Christian scriptures that teach that
God is love? The answer is very clear to those who read the
Bible as one story, not as scattered verses used as proof-
texts to support the gods we make of nation, race, family,
pleasure, and money. From Joshua to Jesus the central
emphasis is on our need to repent and abandon our whole
heart, mind, and soul to God's holy Spirit, trusting completely in his power to deliver us—and seeing the vanity
and folly of putting our hope in human wisdom, schemes,
and systems to deliver us from evil.

*H. Goeringer*

CHRISTIANS MAKE a fatal mistake when they take
their politics from the Old Testament. The politics that the
prophets were continually protesting had become idola-
trous. Even David was not allowed to build a temple of
worship because he was told, "your hands are too bloody."

*H. Goeringer*

*28*   ON THE PAGES of the Bible, God leads us ever
upward from the vengeful mind of the Old Testament to
the merciful mind of the New Testament. To live by the
Mosaic law of retaliation taught and practiced by Joshua,
while professing to be a disciple of Jesus, who taught
perfect love, is not only to continue to live in the darkness
of sin and death but—what is infinitely worse—to prostitute the gospel. It is to put Jesus' hand on the switch that
kills the criminal. It is to put Jesus in the political palaces
of the world, to vote to spend trillions of dollars for
weapons with enough power to completely destroy every
city on the face of our God-created earth. This is salvation?
No! This is the sinner of the Old Testament still yearning
for salvation, still longing to live in the peace of God's
holiness.

*H. Goeringer*

AFTER BEING BOGGED DOWN for forty years in the desert, the children of Israel finally head for the Promised Land. The first population center standing in their way is Jericho. Then, as now, the general in command relied on his CIA for vital information to help Joshua mobilize the marines and devise the best military strategy to get the job done. But the plan of victory came not from the Pentagon:

> On the seventh day you shall march around the city seven times, the priests blowing the trumpets. And when they make a long blast with the ram's horn, as soon as you hear the sound of the trumpet, then all the people shall shout with a great shout; and the wall of the city will fall down flat, and the people shall go up every man straight before him (Jos. 6:4–5).

The strategist is the Lord, not captain Joshua. Israel's manual was not written by the C - I - A but by the S- P- I - R - I - T, which has his way of playing down the military:

> Woe to those who go down to Egypt for help and rely on horses, who trust in chariots because they are many and in horsemen because they are very strong, but do not look to the Holy One of Israel or consult the Lord! (Is. 31:1)

*H. Goeringer*

*30*   GIDEON STARTED with 32,000 soldiers to defeat
Midian. "Too many," said the Lord. "With that much
military power Israel will claim the glory for themselves and
say that it is their own strength that has given victory." So
the ranks are drastically cut to 300. The strategist is the
Lord, not Gideon. What's the point? It's the one and only
point that God is trying to teach a fallen world—the gods
of the nations are idols that cannot save us. The might of
Saul, the arm of David, the wisdom of Solomon are all
vanity. Their deeds are not there for us to emulate, but
there to lead us to repentance—and to Jesus.

*H. Goeringer*

CAN YOU IMAGINE a general saying to his troops,
"Today we're not going to fire a single weapon. We're
going to stay right where we are and not even talk. We're
going to be still and pray, and God will fight for us." The
man's crazy! Must be battle fatigue.

That's exactly what the people of Israel thought when
Moses was leading them out of Egypt. Looking back at the
pursuing armies of Pharaoh that had them hemmed in on
every side, they shouted to Moses, "Better for us to go back
into slavery in Egypt than die here in the wilderness." Then
they heard the words that would be branded permanently
on the consciousness of this Covenant People: "Fear not,
stand firm, and see the salvation of the Lord, which he will
work for you today. The Lord will fight for you, and you
have only to be still" (Ex. 14:13,14).

*H. Goeringer*

## Man's Need for Redemption

LORD OUR GOD, we come into your presence,  
pleading with you to bring the world what it needs, so that  
men may be freed from all their pain and enabled to serve  
you. Let the power of Jesus Christ be revealed in our time.  
For he has taken on our sin that justice might arise on  
earth, that men might have life and might see your  
salvation, which you will bring when the time is fulfilled.  
Let your power be revealed in the world, and let your will  
be done, your name be kept holy, and all wrongs be  
righted in this turbulent and difficult age. O Lord our  
God, you alone can help. You alone are the Savior of all  
peoples. In your great mercy you can bring peace. We look  
to you. And when we consider your Word, we remember  
the mighty promises you have given, promises which are to  
be fulfilled in our time. Amen.

*C. F. Blumhardt* [1]

*34*   VIOLENCE is a terrible reality. It is the consequence of
sin, that is to say, the consequence of our separation from
God. Just as light implies darkness, and beauty has its
opposite in ugliness, and truth is possible only if there is
untruth to choose from, so nonviolence is conceivable only
if violence is a possibility. To live in peace and harmony as
children of God, there must be the possibility of the
opposite kind of life. We are not controlled puppets.
Created in the image of God we have a free will, the
freedom to choose between opposites, between self-will
and God's will, hate and love, war and peace, violence and
nonviolence, Babylon and Paradise. To be human is to
make free choices. Violence is the consequence of wrong
choices.

*H. Goeringer*

THE STORY of Adam and Eve and their rebellion,
which led to "Paradise Lost," is the story of our life today as
person, family, race, and nation. The consequence for us
will be the same as that of the first family. Violence
followed immediately upon their separation from God:
"Cain rose up against his brother Abel and killed him"
(Gn. 4:8).

*H. Goeringer*

*"The whole world is in the power of the evil one"*
(1 Jn. 5:19).

THE CURSE of evil and its death prevails in every
culture and civilization and is not overcome by literacy
campaigns, balanced budgets, military power, college
degrees, better nutrition, radical revolutions, or
democratic elections. This evil that pollutes the very
atmosphere of every culture is not overcome by the success
of some kind of social action out there in the world. Evil's
curse of violence and death can only be overcome in one
place—in the kingdom of God that Jesus Christ initiates
within you and me by the power of his holy love. Then, and
only then, abiding in God's Spirit and living as a citizen of
Christ's eternal kingdom, can we live nonviolently and
witness in every phase of life to the reality of peace that
fulfills all justice and human dignity. It is God's peace that
the world of nation-states can neither give you nor take
from you. It is peace shaped by a cross, a resurrection, and
God's Spirit, which comes to us in Jesus with the Good
News: "Peace be with you. Receive the Holy Spirit" (Jn.
20:21,22).

*H. Goeringer*

*36* WE HAVE TO BELIEVE in the indescribable longing of God's heart to save mankind, not only from its need but also from the terror of its sin. Jesus is the answer, the only answer to sin and to the world need. If God did not have this longing to seek men out and save them, there would be only inner and physical death here. The Gospel of John begins with John the Baptist saying of Jesus, "This is the Lamb of God who will carry the sin of the whole world." It is irreverent to talk only of world need and not to see how God is hurt by our sin, by world sin.

*J. H. Arnold* [2]

WHAT DOES THE WORLD today need? What do the     *37*
men of today need? One thing is clear: we need the
salvation and redemption of Jesus. We know that the
greater part of mankind today is chained and bound in
egoism and sin, but we also know that Jesus Christ loves all
men, and because of this, love toward all men is born in
our hearts. Love to Christ must so drive and urge us that
we give everything to him. He loves mankind and he alone
can redeem it.

*J. H. Arnold* [3]

*38*   SINCE THE 4TH CENTURY the church has rel-
egated Jesus and his peace to the private sector of life,
leaving our collective life in the hands of the state's military
to achieve peace by war and the treaties that follow. Always
seeking their own national interests based on an ethic of
survival, nations are the cause of war. Their peace treaties
that follow are the seeds that produce the next war. The
Treaty of Versailles produced Hitler; the Yalta Peace
Conference produced a continuing war between the Soviet
Union and the United States. Such is the peace that the
world gives and the politicized church allows it to masquer-
ade as peace. Such so-called peace is the age-old sin of a
fallen world.

*H. Goeringer*

AGAIN AND AGAIN, in the life of a nation, between     *39*
nations and in the class struggle, we experience violent
outbursts of accumulated tensions and conflicts. These
outbursts reveal the existing state of mutual exploitation
and oppression, and, last but not least, the savage instincts
of chaotic, covetous passion. This volcanic eruption of
bloodthirsty, inordinate passions and of merciless
countermeasures has intensified and spread.

*E. Arnold* [4]

*40*  **WHY ARE THERE** armed forces? Why are there law courts? Why is there a militia? Undoubtedly they exist simply for the sake of property, that isolated thing which has become detached from all the rest, and which is doomed to death. We must break through this atmosphere of impending disaster. We are lost as long as the main factors in life are man's covetous will, his struggle for existence, his selfish claims, and his selfish rights and privileges. We have fallen into a state of disintegration; we have fallen from God. This curse that lies over us, this ruined life, has become a commonplace fact that we take for granted. We must wake up and hear the gospel which will free us from the curse of this life without spirit and without God.

*E. Arnold* [5]

ONE CANNOT YET SAY that world peace and God's     *41*
peace are assured. They are assured in the deepest sense,
but not in the political sense. Countries are building up
freedom and security on the most dangerous weapon that
ever existed. We, on the other hand, are challenged to
build our security on something else—that which is of
God—and to hope that something happens from God for
all the nations. It is not enough for us to have the most
perfect life of peace in our church. Our longing will not be
satisfied until the whole earth is under the rulership of
God instead of under the rulership of force.

*J. H. Arnold* [6]

42  *"The Lord is my rock, and my fortress, and my deliverer, my God, my rock, in whom I take refuge"* (Ps. 18:2).

IN A WORLD OF SIN people idolatrously believe that security rests with military power. Just look at the futile fortresses in which humanity has placed its trust for security. The Chinese built their Great Wall of 1400 miles back in the third century BC to defend against the nomadic tribes. The French built the Maginot Line, a reproduction in concrete and steel of the deep trench systems of the western front that consumed 150,000 tons of steel, 1.5 million cubic feet of concrete, contained 62 miles of tunnels, and ran the whole length of the Franco-German border. But then came Hitler's bombers and the rock of the Maginot Line was shattered.

Now the name of the rock that the brilliant minds of science have handed to the military for our salvation is called nuclear energy. So, why worry. The President is an OK rock. The Pentagon is an OK rock. The Marines are an OK rock. So, sleep well tonight in the blessed assurance that we're all OK rocks.

*H. Goeringer*

WHAT IS THE ROCK that stands secure so that we will     *43*
not fear? It is the rock upon which Jesus has built his
church: "You are the Christ, the Son of the living God"
(Mt. 16:16). Jesus and his resurrection is God's Maginot
Line poured in the steel and concrete of agape, which is
the same forever.

*H. Goeringer*

DEFENDING their collective egotism, men say: "I don't
want my property for myself, I want it for my wife and
children. I don't in the least want to go to war to protect
my own personal property, but I will fight for the good of
all." A man who loves wife and children loves his own flesh.
Not only love for one's own family, but preservation of the
clan, loyalty of tribesmen or settlers, defense of nation or
state, and still more, civil war or war fought for one's own
caste or class, is collective egotism.

*E. Arnold* [7]

*44*   **SOME OF US** once believed that through political or social measures a radical change could take place. But as one sees today, world leaders get caught up in their own lies and webs of dishonesty. We know that we cannot change the world. Dark powers rule today (I don't mean human beings) and bring injustice and bloodshed and unfaithfulness into the lives of men. But Christ came, and we believe that he, not the President, will one day come again to govern the earth. Ultimately Christ will rule, and for this we live and give everything; for this we are willing to die.

*J. H. Arnold* [8]

LET ME SPEAK frankly: I oppose nationalism and      *45*
patriotism; I oppose the class war of the proletariat; I
oppose the class rule of the property owners; and in
addition I oppose the laws of inheritance. I assert that
egotism rears its head wherever there is any question of
protecting common interests. I oppose the party system.
The whole of our public life has fallen under this curse.

*E. Arnold* [9]

# BE SUBJECT TO
# GOVERNING AUTHORITIES
(ROM. 13:1)

LORD OUR GOD, we wait for you night and day. We    *47*
believe in you and we long for your righteousness. You will
answer our prayer. Bless us, we pray. May your name be
kept holy and your kingdom come. O Lord our God, may
your will be done among the nations. May your will be
done in each of us and be plainly seen in men, as it is in
heaven. Look upon the nations. Watch over all mankind.
Let a new path be broken so that a peace that passes all
understanding may come, a peace from you, the Lord our
God. Amen.

*C. F. Blumhardt* [1]

*48*   FOR ALMOST THREE CENTURIES the early
church submitted to the government and honored the
rulers, but they refused to obey the command of the state
to kill. They did not confuse respecting the state with
worshipping the state. They prayed for the king, but they
did not worship the king. They recognized the authority of
government but did not allow political authority to usurp
the place of God's absolute authority, saying with
Theophilus, "I will rather honor the king, not indeed
worshipping him, but praying for him; but God, the living
and true God, I worship, knowing that thè king is made by
him." [2]

*H. Goeringer*

**GRANT HARMONY** and peace to us and to all the    *49*
inhabitants of the earth . . . Grant this also to those who
rule and govern us on earth. Thou, O Ruler, hast given
them the power of government through thy majesty and
unutterable might so that we, acknowledging the honor
and dignity given to them by thee, may be subject to them
without opposing thy will in anything. Grant to them, O
Lord, health, peace, concord, and firmness so that they
may administer without offense the government which
thou hast given them! For thou, O Heavenly Ruler, King of
the Ages, hast given to the children of men glory and
dignity and authority over the things which are on earth.
Do thou, O Lord, direct their counsels according to that
which is good and pleasing in thy sight so that they may
with reverence exercise the authority thou hast granted
them, peacefully and benevolently, without violence, and
thus obtain thy mercy.

*First Letter of Clement* [3]

*50*  FROM THE TIME of Jesus' resurrection and the birth
of the church at Pentecost until Emperor Constantine's
offer of partnership with the Roman State, rejection of the
sword was a continuing theme of early Christian theology.
This is documented in early catechetical vows forbidding
Christians to engage in killing. Instead of blending in and
living as typical Romans, Christians were persecuted
because their worship of Christ as "Kyrios," Lord of the
whole earth, set them against the state and its demand of
absolute loyalty to the emperor and his commands.

*H. Goeringer*

THE FIRST CHRISTIANS recognized the  *51*
government as a transitory necessity, although they
considered it of but very relative moral value. However, the
fact that these revolutionaries of the Spirit knew that they
were actually the State's best helpers and allies in the cause
of morality and world peace proves that theirs was quite a
positive attitude to the ethical importance of the State.
They realized clearly that, until the time of God's decisive
intervention, they of themselves were unable to change the
structure of the present order. They did not feel able to
bring about any substantial improvement for the masses,
not even in the direction of social reform.

*E. Arnold* [4]

*52*  THE NEW TESTAMENT teaches Christians to obey such laws of the government as stopping at a traffic signal when it is red, not stealing someone else's money, and similar regulations which protect life. But the New Testament teaches Christians to disobey the State when the command of Caesar is to kill and destroy life. At the heart of Jesus' teaching is "Seek first the kingdom of God" (Mt. 6:33). To believe in God is to recognize God as the highest authority of your life, and God's command could not be clearer: "Thou shalt not kill." To believe in the God who revealed himself in Jesus is not only to refuse to kill an enemy, but not even to allow the spirit of hatred to control one's heart and mind, yes, to love an enemy. Blind obedience to the state and its command to kill is practical atheism, no matter what one's record of church attendance on Sunday.

*H. Goeringer*

WE NEITHER WISH nor intend to remove the
governing authority of this world or to disobey it in what is
good and just. There has to be government for the people
in the world just as much as there has to be daily bread.
The masses refuse to be ruled by God's Word. If they were
not bridled and kept within bounds, no one would be safe
from his neighbor, and the earth would be drenched with
blood.

53

Government, therefore, is God-ordained, and we rightly
respect its officials because of their position. We show them
friendliness, obey them, and pay their fees readily and
regularly . . . This a Christian may do as long as it is not
against his faith and conscience.

*Early Hutterite statement* [5]

*54*  THE EARLY CHRISTIANS found it impossible to take responsibility for any penalty or imprisonment, any disfranchisement, any judgement over life or death, or execution of any death sentence pronounced by martial or criminal courts. Several trades and professions were also out of the question for them, or regarded as highly dubious, because they were connected with demonic idolatry and immorality. The unemployment resulting from such renunciation and the ensuing threat of hunger were as frightening as the violent death of martyrdom.

*E. Arnold* [6]

THE PROFESSIONS and trades of those who are going    55
to be accepted into the community must be examined. The
nature and type of each must be established. . . A military
constable must be forbidden to kill. If he is commanded to
kill in the course of his duty he must not take this upon
himself, neither may he swear; if he is not willing to follow
these instructions, he must be rejected. A proconsul or a
civic magistrate who wears the purple and governs by the
sword shall give it up or be rejected. Anyone taking part in
baptismal instruction, or anyone already baptized, who
wants to become a soldier shall be sent away, for he has
despised God.

*Hippolytus* [7]

*56*   WE BELIEVE with the apostle Paul that the governing
authorities are servants of God's wrath. Therefore we pay
taxes and duties, do our share of compulsory labor, and
anything else that is not against our consciences. But if the
governing authorities require anything that destroys peace,
such as war taxes, executioner's dues, or anything to serve
bloodshed, we refuse to support it either by word or deed,
for we know that vengeance belongs to the Lord alone. We
are not to fight evil but to love our enemies.

*Early Hutterite statement* [8]

THERE IS NO STATE that does not have a police    *57*
force to wield the sword. What God has in the state, then,
is an order of the sword's wrath. This is what God has
ordained in the unchristian world so that evil shall not gain
the upper hand. Rape-murderers cannot be allowed to kill
every little girl. That is God's order in hell! God has an
order in hell, an order for the evil and unjust. We must not
forget that. The state and the police force are God's order
in the world of evil, not in the world of good. In the world
of evil God's relativity reigns. We could not stand up in
London now and preach: "Away with all policemen!" We do
not deny the necessity of government order for the world
of evil. That would be an error.

*E. Arnold* [9]

*58*   ROMANS 13:1–5 show what the state's task is: to
punish evil with the sword. In contrast to this, Paul says in
verses 8–10, "Love is the fulfilling of the law. Owe no one
anything, except to love one another." Paul is saying by this
that the Christian way is different from that of the state.
"Love does no wrong to a neighbor." God's absolute is love!
In the sphere of absolute love there is no active participation in the State's violence. In the sphere of God, which is
absolute, there is no police system. There are two regions.
One region is that of evil and of government force. The
other region is that of love and of the Holy Spirit; this
region has no active participation in government force.

*E. Arnold* [10]

ROMANS 13:1–7 does not in any way replace God's **59** law, "Thou shalt not kill." Paul wrote this letter at a time when many groups were opposing the rulers of Rome with violence. Christians who were continually being harassed in one way or another by the Roman authorities, and especially Jews whose native land had been occupied for a long time by Rome, were certainly tempted to resist and join hands with those whose strategy of protest was one of violence. In this letter Paul is advising his friends in Rome not to resist the government with violence. In substance Paul is saying, "Submit to Rome, that uses the sword to execute God's wrath against evil. But you do what is good and you will not have to fear God's wrath that punishes the wrongdoer."

*H. Goeringer*

ROMANS 13:1–7 is not a call for Christians to resist evil with evil and in so doing conform to the mind of a fallen world. Rather it is a call to submit even to an empire like that of Rome and not to engage in bloody slaughter to try to topple it. In a fallen world God allows human governments to exist to prevent complete anarchy.

*H. Goeringer*

*60*   *Testimony of three Anabaptists before Zwinglian priests in Zurich,*
*1575:*

THEY WERE ASKED why men holding government
office cannot be Christians. Brother Ludwig pointed out
that Christ had fled when the people had wanted to make
him king (Jn. 6:15) and that he had refused to be a judge
or divide an inheritance when someone asked him to (Lk.
12:13–14). His followers should do as he did. God ordained
that his chosen ones should conform to the likeness of his
Son, and what is more, Christ says to his own, "In the
world, princes rule over the people, but it shall not be so
with you" (Mt. 20:25–26). "Indeed, they are not to resist
evil, though the men of old had authority to do so by the
law of Moses" (Mt. 5:39). When Jesus' disciples wanted
revenge by calling down fire from heaven as Elijah had
done, he said to them, "You do not know to what spirit you
belong" (Lk 9:54–55).

   Just as Christ did not use either worldly authority or
outward force, no more can a Christian. A man does not
belong to Christ unless he has Christ's spirit, and so no
Christian can be a magistrate in the world. But a magistrate
may well become a Christian if he humbles himself and
flees from his high position, as Christ did, giving his whole
life to good works as the apostle teaches. [11]

IN AN EVIL WORLD separated from God it is the    *61*
nature of the state to use the sword to establish law and
order to be able to survive. Yes, God uses the state to
punish a self-centered world that lives to satisfy its own
comfort and appetites, just as God used Assyria and
Babylonia to punish Israel. In this sense the state is "God's
servant," and does not "bear the sword in vain" (Rom.
13:4). Every sinner, including myself, needs the state to
teach us to live within the framework of the law. But when I
repent of my sinful self and put on the Lord Jesus Christ,
God's reign in Christ has my total allegiance.

*H. Goeringer*

*62*  **CHRISTIANS WHO ARE FIRM** in the faith say "No!"
to the state's command to kill and "Yes!" to Jesus' command to "love your enemies and pray for those who
persecute you" (Mt. 5:44). Jesus—his cross, resurrection,
Holy Spirit—is God's answer to killing and war. Not the
state. Let the church be the church and live once again as
the one world-wide reconciled body of Christ and be the
blessed peacemaker she has been called to be.

*H. Goeringer*


**WE DO NOT GO FORTH** as soldiers with the Emperor
even if he demands this, but we do fight for him by
forming our own army, an army of faith through our
prayers to God.

*Origen* [12]

*A letter to the local governor during a time of persecution, written on*     *63*
*behalf of the Hutterites (early 1530's).* [13]

WE DO NOT WANT to hurt or wrong anyone, not even
our worst enemy, be it Emperor Ferdinand or anyone else,
great or small. All our words and deeds, our conduct, our
way of life, are there for all men to see. Rather than
knowingly wrong a man to the value of a penny, we would
let ourselves be robbed of a hundred gulden. Rather than
strike our worst enemy with our hand—to say nothing of
spears, swords, and halberds such as the world uses—we
would let our own lives be taken.

As anyone can see, we have no physical weapons,
neither spears nor muskets. No, we want to show by our
word and deed that men should live as true followers of
Christ, in peace and unity and in God's truth and justice.

*Jakob Hutter (d.1536)*

*64*   AS PART OF A FALLEN WORLD, nation-states will
continue to legalize war and use war to protect their own
national life and vested interests. This is the nature of
every state and its laws which are grounded in national
pride. But, says the New Testament, "You are not under law
but under grace" (Rom. 6:14). The ministry committed to
us in Christ is to witness to the saving grace of God's love
revealed on the cross, not to give blind obedience to the
state when its command of law is to kill and engage in war
that breaks all of God's moral laws. Engaging in war we live
as children of God's wrath. Engaging in Jesus' ministry of
reconciliation, we live as children of God's love. When we
obey Caesar's command to kill we render unto Caesar the
things that belong only to God. In Caesar's political world
governed by national pride there will continue to be wars
and rumors of war. In God's spiritual kingdom governed by
Jesus' agape-love, war is ended. War is sin, and sin no
longer has any dominion over us. Ours is the peace already
achieved for us by God's mighty acts of salvation in the
death and resurrection of Jesus. War will continue in the
world of the flesh. But war is ended in Christ.

*H. Goeringer*

THE LOVE OF ENEMIES that Jesus commands is not conditional. Jesus is the unconditional standard of the Christian, and the standard of his life and teachings is clear. Our options are to follow or not to follow. To let the state set the standard based on what the world calls practical and realistic is not an option for the Christian. No state is worthy of our absolute allegiance. Nothing is eternal except God.

*H. Goeringer*

*66* AS SPANISH is the language of Latin America and French the language of France, so the language of all governments in the world is the language of the military. When the chips are down and a government believes its existence is threatened, it responds in the only way it knows how—with military force. The history of nation-states is the history of war. It is impossible for a nation-state to follow Jesus to the cross and offer its life in God's self-giving love. The difference between governments that rule by force and the government of the kingdom of God that lives by meekness and humble service is clear in this statement of Jesus: "You know that the rulers of the Gentiles lord it over them, and their great men exercise authority over them. It shall not be so among you; but whoever would be great among you must be your servant, and whoever would be first among you must be your slave; even as the Son of man came not to be served but to serve, and to give his life as a ransom for many" (Mt. 20:25–28).

*H. Goeringer*

CHRISTIANS MUST understand that the peace Jesus    67
talks about is not achieved by pressuring governments to
disarm. This is to attempt to get a government to live as the
kingdom of God, and to act on the premise that what the
Bible means by peace is a goal to be achieved by political
effort in the future. By their very nature governments live
to survive and act within a framework of law designed to
create and preserve a relative degree of order and justice
within their own nation. The life of that nation-state and its
government is based on law which must be enforced by
coercive power resulting one way or another in violence.
There is no such thing as a gentle army or police force.

*H. Goeringer*

*68*    THE KINGDOM OF GOD is life in Christ whose peace is a reality already achieved for us through his cross and resurrection. Jesus does not call us to try to eradicate violence by writing letters to political leaders urging them to vote against a particular bill that calls for this or that weapon. Those with decision-making power in government may or may not vote for the proposed legislation. Never will they vote to disarm the government and live by Jesus' teaching, "Love your enemies, do good to those who persecute you, forgive those who trespass against you, etc." Never, never will the body of the state exclaim, "Far be it from me to glory except in the cross of our Lord Jesus Christ, by which the world has been crucified to me, and I to the world" (Gal. 6:14).

*H. Goeringer*

IN THEIR OPPOSITION to military operations, Christians are not anti-American. Our new life of the Spirit revolves around the politics of the cross and submission to God's plan of reconciliation in Jesus, not in the power politics of the state or military plans to retaliate when threatened or attacked. It would be naive to believe that any state in the world can become a Christian state and follow the Sermon on the Mount. Jesus comes to the individual as the giver of God's Spirit, whose fruit is agape and peace. The only abiding place for God, who is Spirit, is within the mind and soul of the individual.

It is urgent that Christians in every nation understand that no state is holy and worthy of our unconditional allegiance. And it is just as urgent to understand that no church is holy that allows her life to be corrupted by the state and perverts the gospel by identifying the mission of Jesus with the mission of the state and its military system. The time has come for Christians to take their protests to their churches, where we should expect Jesus' nonviolent cross to be proclaimed.

*H. Goeringer*

*70*     IT IS A MATTER of deepest regret that serious-minded
Christians today do not have the simple and clear witness
of Jesus and of primitive Christianity which living biblical
churches and movements in other centuries represented
and proclaimed so strongly. Living Christians who took a
determined attitude in life felt that war and the military
profession are irreconcilable with the calling of
Christianity. There certainly must be police forces today.
The service of such forces is more ethical than the
competition of two business concerns in which only one of
them is able to survive. But what we are concerned with
here is a completely different question: the question of the
mission and testimony of Christ, the question of the
church and the task she has been commissioned to do.

*E. Arnold* [14]


THE DIVINE BANNER and the human banner do not
go together, nor the standard of Christ and the standard of
the Devil. Only without the sword can the Christian wage
war: the Lord has abolished the sword.

*Tertullian* [15]

THE EARLY HUTTERITES practiced Christian          *71*
community of goods as Christ taught it and lived it with his
disciples and as the first apostolic church practiced it.
Those who earlier had been rich or poor now shared one
purse, one house, and one table.

Swords and spears were forged into pruning knives,
scythes, and other tools. There was no musket, saber,
halberd, or any other weapon of defense. Each was a
brother to the other. They were a thoroughly peaceful
people who never took part in any war or bloodshed by
paying war taxes, much less by active participation. They
did not resort to revenge—patience was their weapon in all
strife.

They were subject to the authorities and obedient to
them in all good works, in all things that were not against
God, their faith, or their conscience. They paid their
taxes. They honored the governing authorities because of
their divinely ordained office, which is as much needed in
this wicked world as daily bread.

*Hans Kräl* [16]

72    THE CHRISTIAN CHURCH is the region of absolute
love. In the region of absolute love there is no taking
active part in the force of the State. Only by doing evil
does one leave the region of love that is God's absolute.
Government is instituted by God, but it is at the same time
an instrument of the devil. The church serves but one
Spirit—the absolute God. Every state, however, serves two
spirits because it belongs to evil. On the one hand it serves
God's order, on the other hand, the devil.

*E. Arnold* [17]

## Our Violent Culture

LORD OUR GOD, we come to you, the source of all 
being. Help us to recognize you more and more, so that we
hear you, the mighty One, say, "Stop, O men. Make peace.
No one of you is more important than any other.
Remember that I am God of all, in south and north, in
west and east, on the oceans and everywhere. I am the one
God, and through Jesus Christ I am now your Father."
Amen.

*C. F. Blumhardt* [1]

74 **FROM THE TIME** of their birth, babies imbibe our culture of violence with their mother's milk. As they grow up and watch the game on television, nobody is there to question the commercials paid for by the army telling them that the way to be the best they can be is to join the country's armed forces. Nobody is there to talk about such other-worldly and unrealistic subjects as life in the kingdom of God.

*H. Goeringer*

ONE OF THE FIRST objects a child observes is a gun    75
and its connection with killing. The soldier is one of our
first mental images. National anthems glorifying the nation
are among the first songs memorized in school, along with
the pledge of allegiance to the flag, which implies a
connection between obedience to the state and obedience
to God. The child's first text books tell the story of the
nation held together by the blood-red thread of the
military. We are not talking only about the militarism of the
United States. This is the mark of human civilization from
tribal history to the present hour. The form of government
and the kind of weapons change. The bone and marrow
fighting instinct of the flesh remains the same. It is the
prevailing view of reality on television today as it was the
prevailing view of reality before the alphabet was invented.

*H. Goeringer*

**76**   OUR CULTURE has brainwashed us by teaching children to play with guns and have fun with war toys. In our family album I see my picture at age four, in military uniform, standing with hand on a chair playing General Pershing. As I turn the pages I see two of my brothers in khaki uniform at an army base, training to kill the enemy. I admired them as heroes.

No one ever prompted me to question the war system and its patriotism—not my family, not my church, not my school, not my government. Oh yes, I heard how horrible war is, but I never heard anyone say that Christians are called by God to love the "Huns" and the "Japs," not to kill them. No one person, nor one group of people brainwashed me. The whole fallen world and its culture of violence brainwashed me, as it does every person in every age: "For all that is in the world, the lust of the flesh and the lust of the eyes and the pride of life, is not of the Father but is of the world" (1 Jn. 2:16).

*H. Goeringer*

**IT IS OFTEN** held against us that we cannot possibly count on success with the masses: "Can't you see that the refusal of even a few men to bear arms harms your country and will never achieve practical success anyway?"

We answer that at least we make the masses think. It is our duty to show other nations that there are also those among us who do not want war. There must be such a core of people. The more hatred we tear from our hearts, the more room we will have for joy and other more beautiful things. Ultimately it is a question of our rejecting the works of the devil: service to mammon, falsehood, murder, and impurity. All of these are daily realities in our "civilized world."

We are speaking about something very deep; a personal matter which is at the same time universal. When we take the tension between the works of the devil and the power of God's grace and love seriously, the battle will be won again and again—in our life, in the life of the nations, and among the classes. Christ was sent to us so that his peace and love might reign, so that one day all mankind might be reached—and by the word "man" we include with love *all* human beings.

*E. Arnold* [2]

*78*  THE FAMOUS second century "epistle to Diognetus"
comments on Christians of that period: "It is true they are
'in the flesh' but they do not live 'according to the flesh.'
They busy themselves on earth, but their real citizenship is
in heaven." An epistle written about Christians today and
opened a thousand years from now might read, "The pride
of most Christians was the Empire of America and its
earthly pleasures and comforts, which they busied
themselves with protecting at any cost, in the hope that
they would not have to die and give up such earthly
treasure. But alas, death came even though they were
citizens of America whose church-blessed military genius
extended to the stars above."

*H. Goeringer*

IS THERE ANY HOPE that the organized churches    *79*
around the world will approve a peace-covenant that
rejects all violence and war and witnesses to our new life of
agapic love? No, not organized local churches of
competing denominations, which themselves are divided
and at war with each other. Indeed, the great scandal of
the church is not individual Christians breaking one of the
Ten Commandments from time to time, as dramatized by
TV evangelists. The Great Scandal is the massive support
that the Catholic, Protestant, and Orthodox churches give
to the war system of their nation-states that breaks all of
the commandments day in and day out. With few
exceptions, the organized churches of the world reflect the
national cultures of their little worlds.

*H. Goeringer*

*80* THE FALSE PEACE tradition of the church is a political tradition that interprets peace in terms of international diplomacy, arms agreements, the size of military budgets, military alliances, electing "peace candidates" to office, balance of power, peace through strength, Summit Conferences, democratic government and honest elections, and the like. Within such a political framework of nation-states, Jesus' life and teaching of nonviolence is sheer foolishness. It doesn't make a bit of sense to the mind of government leaders for the simple reason that the nation-state is established on man-made laws which require man-made military devices to enforce them. Nonviolence and nation-states are opposites.

*H. Goeringer*

AN AMERICAN CITIZEN in New York was hit over the head twice because he removed signs against a minority group—in this case against Jews. Although I experienced Nazi Germany only as a boy, I know what it means when one is silent in such matters. Germany was taken over by Hitler because many people didn't dare to protest, didn't want to mix in.

I agree it is dangerous for us to get too involved in politics; it isn't the task of the church. But we can't be silent in our own neighborhood; we simply cannot be complacent and say that it is not our business! We must ask ourselves what is the right way to protest, and witness to love and justice.

*J. H. Arnold, 1968* [3]

*82* WHEN THE CHURCH enters into partnership with the state to defend the nation, it accepts the military system and all the violence that goes with it in conducting what the church defines as a "just war." Since those in government always interpret their own military action as "just," and since the state has about it the aura of holy mystery, the war is interpreted by both sides as the will of God and both sides pray to the same God for victory. The church proclaims Jesus as the Savior of the "world" but goes on supporting the nation's same old system of violence and war, implying that Jesus has not saved the world from the ancient curse of slaughtering one another in the spirit of vengeance. When it comes to the issue of war, the state has more influence on the church than Jesus. All of Jesus' teachings on nonviolence are brushed aside.

*H. Goeringer*

GEORGE ZABELKA served as US Army Air Force chaplain to the crew that dropped the bombs on Hiroshima and Nagasaki. For twenty years following World War II he realized more and more that what he had done and believed as a military chaplain was wrong, and that the only way he could be a Christian was to repent and say publicly, "I'm sorry. I'm sorry for what I have done."

Why is it that for centuries the main branches of the church have given their blessing to the "just war?" Zabelka gives us the answer:

"I was brainwashed! Brainwashed not by force or torture, but by my church's silence and wholehearted cooperation in thousands of little ways with the country's war machine. After I finished chaplaincy school at Harvard, I had my military chalice officially blessed by the then Bishop Cushing of Boston. How much more clearly could the message be given? Indeed, I was brainwashed!"

*H. Goeringer*

*84*  LONG, LONG ENOUGH have Christian men
Borne arms against their brother,
And in the very name of Christ
Have maimed and killed each other.
At last through darkness shimmers light,
Shows paths to liberation;
To serve more bloodshed we refuse
For government or nation.

Lay down your weapons, brothers all!
Take not the sword in hand!
For only so shall one day dawn
God's peace in every land.

World churches tell us fighting is
Our Christian obligation;
We answer that they are to blame
For ruthless desolation.
Had Christendom to God been true,
To this world's gods not kneeling,
The specter had long since been laid,
The wounded world known healing.

*Kees Boeke (1884–1966)* [4]

WHAT HOPE IS THERE that such a peace covenant      *85*
will be made by the church that the world may believe?
The hope is with tiny remnants that seek to be an answer
to Jesus' prayer: "As thou didst send me into the world, so
I have sent them into the world" (Jn. 17:18). The peace-
covenant in Christ depends upon little remnants within the
larger organized churches that know they have been sent,
as Jesus was sent, to be set apart for a holy task, making
them different from a world deeply rooted in national
culture and politics. Consecrated in the truth that in Christ
we have received the oneness of the Holy Spirit in whom
there is no violence, we will keep the covenant of peace in
humility, knowing that this is the work of God's grace.

*H. Goeringer*

# DISCIPLESHIP

LORD JESUS, we look to you on the throne beside your     *87*
Father in heaven and ask that you be Lord of peace in our
hearts. Help us to overcome ourselves again and again and
to remain at peace. Then your will may be done in your
disciples, a power of peace may be around us that goes out
into the whole world, and your name may be glorified on
earth. For you are Lord of peace, and we await you. In
difficult times faith and hope will take hold in our hearts
all the more firmly, to your glory, Lord Jesus. For you will
suddenly come according to your promise as the One who
does God's will on earth among all men. Amen.

*C. F. Blumhardt* [1]

*88* **THE CROSS** is the radicalism of love. The peace of the Sermon on the Mount attacks things at their roots. It gives away to love the last remnants of possession, down to shirt, coat, and cloak. The will to peace gives its whole working strength, undivided, to the total, fully united community. As often as love commands, willingness to sacrifice will quietly double the distance or the working time asked.

*E. Arnold* [2]

**THE CHRISTIAN'S** attitude is not based on one or even several of Jesus' specific teachings. For the Christian, nonviolence is simply God alive in us. We say with the apostle Paul: "It is no longer I who live, but Christ who lives in me" (Gal. 2:20). Christian nonviolence is an attitude of what the New Testament calls the "mind of the Spirit" or the "mind of Christ."

*H. Goeringer*

BECAUSE JESUS HIMSELF radiated in his nature the    *89*
organic unity of all the characteristic traits of the spirit of
the future, it was impossible for anyone to try to tear any
one sentence of his out of its context and set it up by itself
as a law. If anyone places pacifistic action or purity of heart
or any other moral or political demand by itself and uses
this to claim and set up the new, he is on the wrong track.
Certainly it is not possible to take part in God's kingdom
without purity of heart, without vigorous work for peace;
but unless the good tree is planted, the good fruit cannot
be harvested. Unless the change extends to all areas, it is a
lost cause to try to emulate Christ in one sphere only.

*E. Arnold* [3]

*90*    THE SERMON ON THE MOUNT teaches Christians to fight, but not as the world fights. We fight not by slaughtering the enemy to be able to do our thing in our own way. We fight by submitting to the enemy to let the sovereign God whose name is love do his thing in his own way. The way of winning by yielding in God's Spirit of reconciling love applies to marriage, friendship, disputes between persons, and every other aspect of life. The way of yielding to evil, instead of fighting evil with more evil, is the Jesus Way. The Sermon on the Mount is based on this fundamental premise: God is real, God is involved in the battle and is fighting for you and every other person on earth.

*H. Goeringer*

WHAT IS THE LORD fighting for? To establish his     *91*
reign within every living soul. In his reign and Spirit is
peace and justice and perfect freedom. Not to resist evil
with violent force is to submit to God and let his sovereign
power take control. To turn the other cheek is not to turn
your life over to the enemy but to turn your life over to
God and allow his plan to work. If God is the center and
circumference of life and everything in between, what can
be better than to submit every particle of your existence to
his infinite love and unique plan for your life?

*H. Goeringer*

92   ATHANASIUS said about the Christians: "When they hear the teaching of Christ, forthwith they turn from fighting to farming, and instead of arming themselves with swords extend their hands in prayer. In a word, instead of fighting each other, they take up arms against the devil and the demons, and overcome them by their self-command and integrity of soul. These facts are proof of the Godhead of the Savior, for he has taught men what they could never learn among the idols."

*H. Goeringer*

WE CANNOT BEAR to see a man put to death, even
justly! How then can anyone accuse us of murder and
cannibalism? How can we possibly kill anyone when we
cannot even look on, lest we are polluted with the guilt of
murder and sacrilege! How can we possibly kill anyone, we
who call those women murderers who take drugs to induce
an abortion, we who say they will have to give an account
before God one day! We are convinced that with God
nothing goes unexamined, and that the body, after serving
the irrational urges and lusts of the soul, will have its share
in punishment. We have, therefore, every reason to detest
even the slightest sin.

*Athenagoras, in response to a charge of cannibalism:* [4]

94  THROUGH CHRIST God reconciles us and gives us the power of the Holy Spirit to live as one body, that the world may believe that God has truly acted to deliver the world from evil and death. It is impossible for us, who "by one Spirit have been baptized into one body" (1 Cor. 12:13), to kill each other just because we happen to be legal citizens of different countries that have decided to go to war against each other for national interests. As members of the body of Christ that transcends nation, race, and every barrier of sin that separates us, and as citizens of the kingdom of God that uses only the sword of the Spirit to carry on our warfare against the powers and principalities of evil, we make a peace-covenant to be faithful to the mission we have been given.

*H. Goeringer*

WE CAN NEVER HOPE to be united with God and     *95*
with one another because of our good works. Our own
violent thoughts are proof of that. The key to the holiness
that unites us is the two words: "In Christ." To repent is to
have such trust in Christ that we are willing to die with him
on the cross to our old life of unholy idolatry that separates
us from God and from our brothers and sisters around the
world. Then from the cross there will blossom a new life of
the resurrection yielding more and more each day to the
holy spirit of agape, which means living for the sake of
others.

*H. Goeringer*

96  JESUS CAME and disclosed his justice to men, both in
the depths of its nature and in its practical consequences.
He showed them that the justice of the future state must
be of an order completely different from that moralistic
justice of the pious and holy. Through Jesus' own nature,
and by the clear words he spoke, he revealed that God's
justice is a living, growing power that develops organically
within us, a life process that takes place in accordance
with sacred laws of life.

*E. Arnold* [5]

A PERSON CAN DO no greater service to his
fatherland than to dare to live out the unbroken will of
love of Jesus, to keep himself from all litigation, to refrain
from all violence and all harming of his neighbors, and to
seek to lead a simple, genuine and pure life. This does not
mean socialism or pacifism as such, as though these
solutions were of worth in themselves. It is something
much deeper: it is the heart of God as revealed in the cross
of Christ. It is the application of the cross of Christ to all
conditions of life, including political and economic life. It
is the radiation of the future kingdom of God into this
present epoch. In opposition to the present epoch, which
is a world of hell, of the devil and of Satan, a world of
mammon, of untruthfulness, injustice and of murder, each
person must show the future epoch as living and present in
himself: the epoch of peace, the epoch of justice, of love
and of joy, the reign of God for which we pray, "Thy will be
done on earth as it is in heaven. Thy kingdom come" (Mt.
6:10).

*E. Arnold* [6]

*98* PEACE IS OUR SALVATION in the risen and crucified Lord who has given the church the opportunity to share, even now, the first fruits of peace in the kingdom of God, which will be consummated at the end-time of history. God's peace in Jesus has come to us from the beyond, that strange world of the Spirit recorded in scripture. We sense the mystery of the Beyond as we read in Luke's Gospel about Elizabeth and Zechariah who are told that a son will be given to them in their old age—a son "to go before the Lord to prepare his ways, to guide our feet into the way of peace" (Lk. 1:76, 79). Peace! It is not an end in itself. Peace is the fruit of the Spirit enfleshed in the person of Jesus whose only glory was pleasing God by abiding in the Father's will.

*H. Goeringer*

CHRIST, WHO IS WHOLE, wants us whole. He loves    *99*
decisiveness. He loves his enemies more than his half-
hearted friends. He hates his falsifiers more than his
opposites. What he abhors is the lukewarm, the colorless
grey, the twilight, the foggy, pious talking that mixes
everything up and commits one to nothing. He sweeps all
that away whenever he draws near.

*E. Arnold* [7]

*100*   GOD'S HEART appeared in Jesus; and to God's heart Jesus consecrates the future. All those who in Christ believe in the future of God's heart are from now on committed to the total will for peace, at any time, in any place.

*E. Arnold* [8]

HIS HEART is his honor. It is *love.* It turns toward all men in the joy of giving. Love is God's honor. His justice is love. To strive solely and exclusively for God's kingdom and his justice brings about in us such a love for all men that we want the same for them in all things as we want for ourselves. This alone is justice: to give up our lives for love.

*E. Arnold* [9]

IF THERE IS one verse of scripture that clearly approves     *101*
our peace-covenant in Christ not to kill one another, it is
John 18:36: "My kingdom is not of this world; if my
kingdom were of this world, my servants would fight, that I
might not be handed over to the Jews." It is important to
understand that Jesus is not only saying as clearly as it can
be stated, "Citizens of my kingdom do not fight." Even
more convincingly, Jesus is practicing what he preaches.
Refusing to fight in self-defence, Jesus is demonstrating
the gospel that proclaims the good news of reconciling
agape that has overcome the self-seeking and death of
Pilate's kingdom of coercive power.

*H. Goeringer*

*102*  THE SO -CALLED peacemaking of nation-states is to glorify nations and their leaders. The peacemaking of the disciples of Jesus is to glorify God. Peace is God's gift in Christ, not the achievement of nations nor the political process. There is no peace in the glory of nations and their military might—there never was, there is not now, and there never will be. The greatest tragedy of the churches is that they have become part of the military systems of the world that blind humanity to the glory of the one God and Father of us all—contrary to Jesus' prayer: "They are not of the world, even as I am not of the world" (Jn. 17:16). Nothing is more a part of our unbelieving world than the military systems of nation-states used to protect what they have and, if possible, to get more wealth and power. It is to this system of sin that our peace-covenant in Christ says, "No!"

*H. Goeringer*

WHERE DOES a young Christian find the answer to the     *103*
question, "Can I as a Christian join the military and kill?"
In the teachings of Jesus, in the life of Jesus himself. "I am
the way, and the truth, and the life" (Jn. 14:6). The good
news is heard when we start with the example of Jesus
instead of the old example of the world's fallen state. Jesus
made crystal clear the nature of his Spirit when he said to
the disciples, "I am gentle and lowly in heart" (Mt. 11:29).
That the first apostles understood Jesus to be a meek and
gentle person is clear in Paul's letter to the church at
Corinth in which he entreats his friends, "by the meekness
and gentleness of Christ" (2 Cor. 10:1). By no stretch of
the imagination do meekness and militarism go together,
as any CIA manual will prove. In battle you either kill or
are killed. Jesus said, "The thief comes only to steal and
kill and destroy; I came that they may have life, and have it
abundantly" (Jn. 10:10).

*H. Goeringer*

*104*   WHEN THE JAPANESE invaded China, Christian
missionaries in Nanking gave New Testaments to the
Japanese soldiers. At first the officers were glad for their
men to have them, but later they came to the missionaries
and said, "Please don't give our men any more New
Testaments. When they read this book, it takes the fight
out of them. They don't want to fight any more."

*H. Goeringer*

AT THE MOMENT when Jesus died, he embraced all   *105*
space and all time; he embraced every millennium and
every nation. He broke down all barriers. He broke down
the barriers between the years. He broke down the bound-
aries between ages and eternities. He broke down the
barriers between the continents. He broke down the
barriers between names, between peoples and nations. He
broke down the barriers of walls and little fences, the
barriers between the individual souls of men. He overwhelmed all time and space with the abundance of his
love. And in this love he brought unity and truth and love
to all men.

*E. Arnold* [10]

*106*   WE DO NOT DENY evil and sin, we do not deny the
end of the world. But we believe in God and his end of the
world, we believe in the rebirth of the earth and of
mankind. This faith is not evolutionism, a belief in the
inevitable ascent to ever greater, more visible perfection.
On the contrary, this faith believes in the growth of the
divine seed in the consciences of men, in the Christ-spirit,
in the rebirth of the individual, in the fellowship of the
church. But it also believes in the upheaval of world
catastrophe, of world judgement in war, revolution and
other horrors of the end; it believes in the collapse of this
depraved and degenerate world of compulsion and
coercion.

*E. Arnold* [11]

JESUS KNEW that he would never be able to conquer   *107*
the earth spirit by greater violence, but only by greater
love. This is why he overcame the temptation to somehow
seize power over the kingdoms of this earth. He
proclaimed the rulership of God, which is of the present
and of the future at the same time. God's will was present
in his life, in his deeds, his words, and in his suffering.
This is why, in his Sermon on the Mount, he speaks of
men who are strong by love, of the peacemakers, of the
men of the heart, who will inherit the land and possess the
earth, to whom the kingdom of God belongs. He took up
the ancient proclamation of peace, the ancient message of
justice, which belongs to the future kingdom of God. He
deepened the crucial word of life: "Thou shalt not kill,"
which rules out murder in every instance, because it is the
original, the very first sacrilege against life. He shows men
that any cruel handling, any brutal violation of the inner
life of men, falls under the same word: it injures body and
soul, yes, God, just as much as the killing of the body.

*E. Arnold* [12]

*108*  THE NUCLEAR AGE that has come upon us compels the church to wrestle as never before with this question: Is it possible for a human being to live in Christ and to share fully in the divine nature of God's spirit of agape, and at the same time, machine-gun mothers and their children and drop bombs on kindred human beings they do not even see? Are these two realities compatible? Following Jesus' resurrection the answer of the early church is clearly expressed in the words of the apostle James: "No, whoever becomes a friend of the world and wages war is an enemy of God" (Jas. 4:4). And the apostle John put it even more strongly: "If anyone says, 'I love God,' and hates his brother, he is a liar; for he who does not love his brother whom he has seen, cannot love God whom he has not seen" (1 Jn. 4:20).

*H. Goeringer*

WE SPEAK UP in protest against bloodshed and *109*
violence, no matter from which side these powers of death
may come. Our witness and our will for peace, for love at
any cost, also at the cost of our own lives, has never been
more necessary than it is today. Those are in error who
reproach us that, at a time when this question is not at all
urgent, we are speaking of defenselessness, nonviolence,
conscientious objection, of discipleship of Jesus in the
power of radiating love, which makes all violence
impossible and excludes us from inflicting any kind of
injury on others. This question is more urgent today than it
ever was, and it will become evident that loyal perseverance
in an attitude of absolute love requires ultimate courage,
manly courage unto death.

*E. Arnold* [13]

*110*  THERE WILL BE VIOLENCE and war in the world
until human history ends, just as there will be every other
kind of sin—adultery, stealing, greed, jealousy, etc. But this
does not give Christians permission to commit adultery,
steal, lie, or engage in war. This is precisely the problem of
our self-obsessed life in our fallen world, and God acted
decisively in the cross and resurrection of Jesus to offer us
his answer to the problem of sin. Listen to the scriptures:
"So you also must consider yourselves dead to sin and alive
to God in Christ Jesus. Let not sin therefore reign in your
mortal bodies, to make you obey their passions" (Rom.
6:11). Violence is sin, a sin to which Christians are dead.

*H. Goeringer*

**WE MUST BE WON** for a great and burning love. I
have to think of the enormous injustice, coldness and
brutality of today. Mankind has seen terrible injustice and
murder since the turn of the century: the First World War,
the communist revolution, Mussolini's fascism, and the
brutalities of Hitler. The murderous injustice in the race
question was so very horrible under Adolf Hitler that it
should have been a warning for all time. Then came
Hiroshima, the cold war, and the wars in Korea and
Vietnam, and Israel. When we visualize all this, we
recognize that it is neither the kingdom of justice nor the
kingdom of peace. This should bring us to an urge, a
longing for God's kingdom.

*J. H. Arnold* [14]

*112*   THE PRIMARY peace witness of the church is not for
or against a nuclear freeze, not supporting or opposing the
deployment of nuclear weapons, not cutting off or
increasing support of terrorists. No, the unique witness of
the church is the proclamation by word and deed of the
one reconciled body of Christ in whom we live and move
and have our being—our new life of agape that says "No"
to all weapons, "No" to all killing, "No" to the whole
military system that demands absolute control of the
individual, "No" to all war. As part of the body of Christ we
say "Yes" to agapic suffering for the redemption of the
enemy. We will not cooperate with the state's retaliation
against the enemy and cause suffering, but say "Yes" to a
shared life of love in Christ so that all of God's children
receive from the church both the justice of food for the
stomach and the risen Christ, whose spirit of eternal life is
food for the soul.

*H. Goeringer*

THE MOST POWERFUL ENEMY of life is death.                    *113*
Because of this we are against the killing of people. We
know that in and of itself it is of little significance whether
a person dies today or after thirty years, assuming that he is
inwardly mature enough for eternity. But we know that
death is something with so much force, something that
sweeps away and clears away; thus we yield the power over
death and life to God alone. We ourselves do not wish to
presume to shorten the life of a human being. We do not
wish to commit a crime against the life created by God.
And if we believe that death is the last enemy, whom Christ
overcame, then we shall not offer him our hand by killing
men.

*E. Arnold* [15]

*114* SO DEAR TO ME, beloved homeland,
Are thy green meadows and thy shore,
Abundant gifts bestowed by God's hand—
No place on earth could I love more.
May no man's hand with blood defile thee,
Nor thy serenity e'er cease;
To war I'll never let them send me,
Courageous be, O land of peace.

Homeland dear, land of peace,
Let every shore from east to west
And all thy sons with peace be blest.

So dear to me, beloved homeland,
Are all thy beauties and thy charms,
That out of love to thee I cannot
Take part in war—I bear no arms.
And should some say that war protects thee,
That for thy good the men are slain,
I say it freely, they are lying:
'Tis not for thee—alone for gain.

*Kees Boeke* [16]

WE EASE OUR conscience by saying the destruction of   *115*
nuclear firepower has become so great that no nation
would dare give the order to press the button. This is the
mistaken logic of "just war" philosophy—the belief that
people act rationally when their nation is threatened. As
we see in the completely irrational acts of terrorists, there
is no reason to believe that small groups of fanatics whose
reading material does not include pastoral letters from
bishops will not learn how to produce nuclear firepower
and use it to achieve their own revolutionary goals. In the
coming of the Nuclear Age, which has put in the hands of
creatures the power to destroy creation, something
radically new has happened that calls Christians to open
their hearts and minds to God's radical new creation in
Christ.

*H. Goeringer*

*116*    *"You will know the truth, and the truth will make you free"*
(Jn. 8:32).

WHAT IS IT that sets human beings free? A violent
American Revolution in 1776? A violent Russian Revolution
in 1917? Not according to Jesus. This is his revolutionary
proclamation of freedom: "Come and learn of me, and I
will make you free." Jesus calls us to the most radical
revolution the world has ever known. Political revolutions
change the external structures of the state. Jesus'
revolution changes the internal nature of the person. One
is a revolution of law that lives in the flesh and is guarded
in fear by force and violence. The other is a revolution of
agapic love that lives in the Spirit who is eternal and needs
not the protection of the flesh. Jesus was talking about a
different freedom and a different consciousness.

*H. Goeringer*

THE FACT THAT people try to live simultaneously on     *117*
the basis of the law and on the basis of grace; that a life of
nonviolence in this age is called fiction, humbug, and
vapor, whereas Jesus, after all, went this way; that people
fight against an uncompromising stand and think that by
doing so they oppose both legalism and fanaticism; that
they say an unqualified "Yes" to the sphere of earthly life;
that they are actually infatuated with the shadow of evil
and take pains to show that one can never get rid of this
shadow, and that basically it makes no difference whether
there is more compromise or less compromise—all this
shows how far off the way they have strayed.

*E. Arnold* [17]

# LOVE YOUR ENEMY
(Mt. 5:44)

**LORD OUR GOD,** bring us men together as one. Give    *119*
us your Spirit so that we may know you, so that joy may fill
our hearts, not only for ourselves but also for others. Root
out evil from the earth. Sweep away all that offends you, all
lying, deceit, and hate between nations. Grant that men
may come to know you, so that disunity and conflict may be
swept away and your eternal kingdom may arise on earth
and we may rejoice in it. For your kingdom can come to
men even while on earth to bring them happiness and to
make them your own children. Yes, Lord God, we want to
be your children, your people, held in your hand, so that
your name may be honored, your kingdom may come, and
your will be done on earth as in heaven. Amen.

*C. F. Blumhardt* [1]

*120*   *"Bless those who curse you, pray for those who abuse you"*
(Lk. 6:28).

WHEN Corrie ten Boom was in a Nazi concentration
camp in Germany she saw her sister Betsie wither away and
die. Betsie was convinced that the terrible hatred they
were experiencing could only be overcome by God's love.
"We must tell people there is no pit so deep that God is
not deeper still. They will listen to us, Corrie, because
we've been here."

So when Corrie got out of the concentration camp she
traveled through Europe and the United States with the
good news of God's love and forgiveness.

One day at a church service in Munich, Germany, she
saw him sitting in the audience. It was the former S.S. man
who had stood guard at the shower room door where it
was decided who was to die and who was to live a little
longer. At the sight of her jailer, all the painful memories
came back to overwhelm her. At the end of the service the
man came up to her beaming and bowing. "How grateful I
am for your message, Fräulein," he said, "To think that, as
you say, he has washed my sins away."

As he reached out to shake Corrie's hand, she kept hers
at her side—she who had been preaching the need to
forgive. Angry, vengeful thoughts boiled up within her. But
then she realized that this is the sin that God's love seeks
to overcome. Yes, Jesus Christ had died for her jailer and

those who killed her sister. She prayed, "Lord Jesus, forgive me and help me to forgive him." Corrie struggled to raise her hand. She breathed another prayer, "Jesus, I cannot forgive him. Give me your forgiveness." As she took his hand the most incredible thing happened. From her shoulder along her arm and through her hand a current seemed to pass from her to him, and a love for her enemy filled her heart that overwhelmed her completely. In that moment Corrie ten Boom discovered that the forgiveness and love that heals and reconciles is the mercy and goodness that springs from the very heart of God in Jesus. Jesus not only tells us to forgive our enemies, he gives us the Spirit that empowers us to do it.

*H. Goeringer*

*122* LOVE SURPASSES all things. It admits no other
emotion. Love permeates hidden prayer as forgiveness. It
determines public conduct when the will for total
reconciliation is absolute, embracing even the enemy—yes,
him in particular. Rather than ever returning curses and
hatred, injury and enmity, whether singly or collectively, it
never takes the slightest part in hostility, quarreling, or war.

*E. Arnold* [2]

LOVE IS NOT influenced by any hostile power. The
attitude of Jesus or his follower cannot be changed by any
turn in a situation. No matter what happens, he only *loves,*
he practices only *peace;* he wishes, requests, and does only
good. Where the peace of Jesus Christ dwells, war dies
away, weapons melt, and hostility dissolves. In Jesus, love
becomes boundless; it becomes sovereign.

*E. Arnold* [3]

THE LOFTIEST HEIGHTS of the spirit that *123*
government can achieve is that of eros, the reciprocal love
that says, "I will love you if you will love me." The kingdom
of God that Jesus inaugurated and proclaimed, on the
other hand, lives by the love revealed on the cross. So
unique is God's love in Christ that the New Testament
writers had to use a new word for it—agape. Agape is love
that gives without counting the cost and asking, "What's in
it for me?" Agape is the love that is willing to suffer, even
for enemies who kill the hand reaching out to help. Agape
is the love that desires above all else to be reconciled
without the desire to dominate. Agape is the love that is
willing to die for others but will never kill others. Agape is
God's eternal Spirit whose fruit is peace, a peace that is
nonviolent.

*H. Goeringer*

*124*    UNCOMPROMISING LOVE has nothing to do with
softness or flabbiness, nothing to do with a passive attitude.
On the contrary, the resolute will for peace has to carry on
a fight of the spirits against all spiritual powers that are
opposed to peace and love. In this fight it is out of the
question to injure or kill one's fellowmen, for the very
reason that no human judgment can judge them as
ultimately evil, as finally rejected, as forfeited to death. All
the more sharply must this fight of the spirits be waged
against everything within us that we recognize to be
inimical or injurious to life, hostile to fellowship, or
directed against God.

*E. Arnold* [1]

GOD, WHOSE agape spirit Jesus reveals on the cross, is     *125*
eternal. Therefore resurrection follows the cross as
inevitably and naturally as dawn follows the darkness of
night. Herein is the key to Christian nonviolence. The key
is not a moral teaching of Jesus, "Love your enemies." The
key is the revelation of God's nonviolent agape spirit in the
person of Jesus and God's act of salvation. Nonviolence has
its beginning and end in the enemy-loving spirit of Jesus.
Not in our moral striving. It is for this reason that Jesus'
nonviolent cross can never be exemplified in the policies
of state. The way of the state and the way of the cross move
in different directions and cannot converge.

*H. Goeringer*

*126*  BIBLICALLY SPEAKING, salvation is the willingness
to change our lifestyle, to change our way of thinking
about the real meaning of our life, to turn from idol
worship—the idols of blood- and material- and nation-
centered relationships and loyalties to a new life of the
Spirit. At the heart of this conversion experience is the
discovery of the nature of God's enemy love that begins to
live in us and control our life as we are saved from the sin
of violence. Now we realize for the first time what the Bible
means: "Beloved, if God so loved us, we also ought to love
one another" (1 Jn. 4:11). When Jesus says, "Love your
enemies and pray for those who persecute you" (Mt. 5:44),
he is simply saying that we are to love one another, even
our enemies, in the same way God loves us. The way of
enemy love (and this includes those the state calls
enemies) is the way of the cross.

*H. Goeringer*

YES, THIS IS God's peace plan: to unite all in Christ!     *127*
When we live in Christ we love our enemies and overcome
evil with the good spirit of God he gives us.

*H. Goeringer*

THE CROSS IS the agape-bridge that brings us
together, forgiving our self-love and creating in us a new
life of God-love and brother-sister-love even when our
brothers and sisters are hostile to us, even when one of our
brothers is Khadafy and uses the sword of the flesh that
kills. Christians are to act toward the Khadafys of the world
in the Spirit of the same redemptive love that reaches out
to us from a cross even while we mock and spit and drive
the spear into Jesus' body. In one way or another we are all
terrorists until God's redeeming love in Christ overcomes
our hostility.

*H. Goeringer*

*128*   ASK PAUL, the clearest writer and most influential
preacher in the early church, about peace. His witness has
no conditions: "He is our peace" (Eph. 2:14). Ask Paul how
to deal with enemies, and his answer is precisely the gospel
of Jesus: "If your enemy is hungry, feed him; if he is thirsty,
give him drink. Do not be overcome by evil, but overcome
evil with good" (Rom. 12:20, 21). Ask Paul about the kind
of weapons to use in waging war against evil, and he
answers: "The weapons of our warfare are not worldly." He
lists them one by one in his letter to the church at
Ephesus: "Truth, righteousness, the gospel of peace, faith,
salvation, the sword of the Spirit, prayer." Four words say it
all: "He is our peace."

*H. Goeringer*

**ON THE CROSS,** God's revolution is still going on as he    *129*
seeks to change us from hostile enemies to reconciled
friends. "Estranged and hostile in mind, doing evil deeds"
(Col. 1:21). That's us. You and me. The Bible says, "While
we were enemies we were reconciled to God by the death of
his Son" (Rom. 5:10). Even as we snarl and spit at him, God
in Jesus reaches out to us in suffering love, pleading with us
to end the hostility and enmity and accept his offer of
peace. This is the way God loves us. This is agape, God's love
revealed in Jesus. God so loves an enemy world fallen into
worship of self, family, money, and nation that he gives
himself in Jesus that we might not perish but have
everlasting life (Jn. 3:16). There is nothing more that God
can do to keep us from destroying ourselves. God's forgiving
and reconciling love is offered to us from a cross even
while we live in our self-will as his enemies—if this is not
enough we are doomed to defeat and destruction.

*H. Goeringer*

*130*     IF THERE IS one thing the Bible makes clear it is that
one proves true one's relationship to God by one's
relationship to other people. This is what Jesus is teaching
in Matthew 25:34–40—when we show love to those in
need, we show love to him. The reverse is also true. When
we show violence toward other people, we show violence
toward him. Jesus taught his disciples to pray: "Forgive us
our trespasses as we forgive those who trespass against us"
(Mt. 6:12), which means that God's love is able to forgive
our sin and renew us in his spirit only as we show love to
our enemy and forgive him. Love of God and love of
neighbor are two sides of the same coin. They cannot be
separated.

*H. Goeringer*

WHAT DOES the resurrection of Jesus have to do with       *131*
peace? Everything! Jesus' resurrection means that he has
conquered the enemy within us, thereby opening up a
new kingdom of the Spirit that has no use for the military
systems of the nation-states in a fallen world: "In the world
you have tribulation; but be of good cheer, I have overcome the world" (Jn. 16:33). The power of evil and death
was overcome by the resurrection of Jesus, proving that
love of enemies is the way God conquers by his spirit: "Not
by might, nor by power, but by my Spirit, says the Lord of
hosts" (Zec. 4:6).

When Jesus said, "I am the resurrection and the life"
(Jn. 11:25), he was proclaiming the new creation—the new
life of the Spirit that is our salvation. In this kingdom of
God established by Jesus there is no death and no need of
armies and their weapons to defend us from death. For
Christians the victory that brings peace has already been
won: "The sting of death is sin, and the power of sin is the
law. But thanks be to God, who gives us the victory through
our Lord Jesus Christ" (1 Cor. 15:56).

*H. Goeringer*

# MARTYRDOM

LORD GOD, we thank you for giving us light here on
earth, where it is so often completely dark. But in the
darkness the name of Jesus Christ shines out as the
prophetic Word: "Be comforted. After darkness comes
light, after night comes day!" We thank you for this light.
In joy we thank you, for we have experienced that Jesus
lives and comes to meet each one, bringing victory over
enemy powers. In the name of Jesus Christ and in his name
alone we ask you to remember the needs of our time. We
do not want anything that comes from ourselves. We do
not want any earthly peace. We want your peace, Lord God,
the peace in which everything becomes new, born anew
even in suffering, to the eternal glory of your name. Amen.

*C. F. Blumhardt* [1]

*134*   *"Now I rejoice in my sufferings for your sake, and in my flesh I
complete what is lacking in Christ's afflictions for the sake of his
body, that is, the church" (Col. 1:24).*

WHAT A DARING thought! Bound in chains in a
prison cell about 60 AD, Paul rejoices in his suffering
because he regards voluntary suffering necessary for
carrying out the mission of the church. American churches
expect to prosper and be happy in nice houses in nice
neighborhoods, not to suffer. But the word "nice" is not
found in the New Testament. The word "suffer" is found
again and again.

It is in the Christ-like willingness to suffer to redeem the
enemy, rather than retaliate to destroy the enemy, that we
have a clue to Christian nonviolence. Like Paul, we must
be willing to suffer and die for the salvation of opponents,
and by so doing show them God's way of the cross that
ends in resurrection.

*H. Goeringer*

**THE MAN WHO** is permeated with life and gripped by    *135*
love is a fighter to the point of shedding his blood. He is
never hard toward his fellow men, though it may be felt as
hardness when in the passion of glowing love he struggles
in volcanic exuberance against the evil he meets within
himself, in his fellow men, and in public affairs. On the
one hand, his fight is a private matter . . . of deepest
mutual relationship between him and God alone; on the
other, it is a very public matter in which he must take a
determined stand in opposition to all human conditions as
they are.

*E. Arnold* [2]

*136*  THE PERFECT PEACE which appeared in Jesus Christ
and his church must, in accordance with the prediction of
the prophets, be attacked by all the powers of world
economy and by all national governments with their
sharpest and deadliest forces. Glowing all the more surely
and clearly, the character of unconditional peace delivers
its bearers defenseless to the flaming sword of their
opponents. Jesus' Sermon on the Mount presents the
sharpest prophecy of the kingdom of peace: readiness to
suffer every death, which is the resistance of the will to
peace. Against the peace-breaking violence of the whole
world it puts up the passive resistance of the cross. The
cross against the sword!

*E. Arnold* [3]

WE WHO ONCE murdered one another not only
refrain from all hatred of our enemies, but more than that,
in order to avoid lying or deceiving our examining judges,
we meet death cheerfully for confessing to Christ.

*Justin* [4]

SOMETHING TREMENDOUS happened in the
resurrection of Jesus. The New Testament makes clear that
for the early church the resurrection of Jesus meant the
world had been turned upside down. Everything became
entirely different because the risen Jesus was now ruling
and the real enemies of evil and death had been van-
quished. The resurrection gave the first Christians the
courage to stand before all the oppressing powers of the
world and call their bluff, as we hear John doing while a
captive on the prison island of Patmos: "Now the salvation
and the power and the kingdom of our God and the
authority of his Christ have come, for the accuser of our
brethren has been thrown down. . . They have conquered
him by the blood of the Lamb and by the word of their
testimony, for they loved not their lives even unto death"
(Rev. 12:10–11). The kingdom of God had come within
them. Their real world was not the ground they walked on
but the Spirit in which they walked.

*H. Goeringer*

*138*   IT WAS IN A nastier world than ours that Jesus said, "Love your enemies, do good to those who hate you, bless those who curse you, pray for those who abuse you" (Lk 6:27–28). Jesus comes to us with God's solution to evil, not in some ideal world when everyone is on their best behavior, but when terrorism is as real as it was when "mad-dog" emperors like Nero used Christians as torches in the gardens of Rome. So far no Christian documents have been uncovered from that time saying, "It's a nasty world. Let's forget Jesus' sentimental sword of love and use the only sword mad emperors understand—the sword that kills. We have suffered enough." No, Peter who is said to have been crucified head down because he felt unworthy to die like his Lord, saw the nastiness of an evil world as an opportunity to use God's sword of the Spirit with the skill he had learned from Jesus. Listen to the scripture a militaristic church seems never to have heard: "For to this you have been called, because Christ also suffered for you, leaving you an example, that you should follow in his steps. When he was reviled, he did not revile in return; when he suffered, he did not threaten" (1 Pet. 2:21,23).

*H. Goeringer*

THE MIGHTY MOVEMENT of the peaceful Ana-
baptists during the time of the Reformation was, above all,
realistic. They never believed that world peace or a gentle
springtime was on the way. On the contrary, they believed
that the day of judgment was at hand. They considered the
Peasants' War to be a powerful warning of God to the
ruling authorities.

This realism, which was aware that the world will always
use the sword, was combined with their firm, clear knowl-
edge that Jesus could never be an executioner. He, who
himself was executed on the cross, could never execute
another. He had killed no one, though he himself was
crucified. The Anabaptists defined the love of Jesus as the
love of the one who, crucified with murderers, could
himself never be a murderer or executioner.

*E. Arnold* [5]

*140* AS THE CIVIL WAR raged, with brother killing brother, Seth Loflin refused to shoulder a gun when he was called up for military service. He said it was against his Christian faith. But the officers, who also considered themselves Christians, promptly put Seth in prison. Finally he faced a court-martial. "Seth Loflin, this court is unanimous in finding you guilty of the gravest insubordination. You will be suspended by your thumbs for one hour."

After the dreadful hour was over, his body worn out, Seth was left to crawl back to his tent. Some of the soldiers felt sorry for him and begged him to change his mind. "Thank you for your kindness, fellows," he said, "but I can't disobey Christ." So he was sentenced to die.

On the appointed day and hour, company after company marched to the parade ground to witness the execution. The firing squad took their places and loaded their rifles. Then the prisoner was brought in. Seth's hands were tied and his eyes were bandaged. Just before the command to fire was given, Seth asked, "May I have a moment or two to pray, sir?" The officer hesitated, but then stepped aside and granted the request.

After several minutes of silence, Seth spoke loudly enough for all to hear, "Father, forgive them, for they know not what they do." There was complete silence. The officer shouted, "Prepare to fire!" Six rifles were shouldered. But when the order, "Fire!" was given, the rifles wobbled downward. Nobody fired.

White with fury, the officer shouted, "What do you think you are doing?" "We can't shoot him, sir," said one of the men. A wave of approval from the soldiers passed through the parade ground.

The death sentence was later canceled, but Seth died in the hospital because of the punishment he had suffered. Having put on the armor of God, Seth was able to refuse the military command to kill his brothers. The Supreme Commander that Seth Loflin obeyed had given a different order: "Love your enemy."

*H. Goeringer*

*142*  DURING WORLD WAR I there was no provision for conscientious objectors to military service in the United States. The following story, as told by Mennonite J. Ewert, tells of four Hutterite brothers who suffered for holding their faith higher than the demands of the state.

Upon their arrival at the military camp in Lewis, Washington, the four Hutterites were asked to sign a card promising obedience to all military commands. As absolute objectors to all military service on the basis of their religious convictions, they refused any service within the military. Therefore the four men were put in the guard house. They were condemned by the court-martial to thirty-seven years and were to serve their term in the military prison on the island of Alcatraz in San Francisco Bay.

Chained together two by two, hands and feet, they were sent there under the guard of four armed men. By day the fetters on their ankles were unlocked, but never the handcuffs. At night they had to lie two by two, flat on their backs, doubly chained together. Upon their arrival at Alcatraz their own clothes were taken from them by force. They were ordered to put on the military uniform, which they refused to do. Then they were taken to the dungeon into dark, dirty, stinking cells for solitary confinement. The uniforms were thrown down next to them with the warning, "If you don't give in, you'll stay here till you die,

like the four we dragged out of here yesterday." So they
were locked up wearing nothing but their light underwear.
Their cell was below sea level, and the water oozed through
the walls.

*After several months of such treatment Joseph and Michael Hofer
died in a military hospital, martyrs for their faith.*[6]

*144*   ASKED WHAT HE would do if he were a German
Christian in the face of Nazi treatment of Jews, Clarence
Jordan replied, "I would put a Star of David on my arm and
get in the concentration camp with them." That's precisely
what he did in the 1940s in Georgia, when black people
continued to suffer at the hands of the KKK and of an
apartheid society. With another family, the Jordans bought
a farm, called it Koinonia, and invited persecuted blacks to
become part of the God-Movement, as Clarence called it.
Together, they resisted evil with the power of Jesus' agape
love—the only power that Jesus teaches his disciples to use.

*H. Goeringer*

# THE KINGDOM OF GOD

**LORD ALMIGHTY GOD,** your name will be
honored. Your kingdom will come for all nations. Your
reign will come over all peoples, for they are all yours and
must acknowledge that Jesus Christ is the Lord, to your
honor, O Father. Amen.

*C. F. Blumhardt* [1]

*146*   OUR WILL and resolution for peace has meaning only
in the determined, certain expectation of Christ's
approaching arrival. Everything else is meaningless.

Looked at historically, our aim in educating others to
this point of view has only a very relative significance;
considered eschatalogically, however, it is of tremendous
significance whether the spirit of this future is present in
some way. The important question is this: "in which epoch
or era have we been placed—the Ice Age? the Stone Age?
the Age of Peace? What hour does the hand of the clock
show? Christ came to give us one common thought—that
is, himself—at the right time. We gather to await his
return. So do the Jews, as they await their Messiah.

In this certainty of expectation we must act in keeping
with its coming. When our faith and our love are strong
enough, unexplained sparks will arise from humanity, so
that when war threatens a united mass will suddenly say,
"No!" The deed is always more important than the
declaration of the deed. As Christ said, "The world shall
recognize you as my disciples by your love to one another."

*E. Arnold* [2]

GOD DID NOT ACT in Jesus to protect our little old     *147*
kingdoms of nation, property, and other accumulated
treasures on earth. He acted on the cross to save us from
these idols and to empower us to live as citizens of his
eternal kingdom. This new Christ-life of the Spirit can be
lived within any political system and does not kill to get the
right system to live in. Killing is contrary to the very nature
of the Spirit. There is no question that the Christian life of
the Spirit will have to endure suffering the greater the
control of the state. But the Christian cannot kill to get the
best system in which to live by love. One contradicts the
other. In the kingdom of God, the end and the means to
the end are one and the same. Both are agape!

*H. Goeringer*

*148*   THE ANSWER TO the need of the world lies in the love of Jesus, which alone can penetrate the world. Human movements such as the Civil Rights Movement are wonderful: people make sacrifices for the sake of righteousness; and some even sacrifice their lives. We must have great respect for them. But the fight for rights will not, in the end, bring the kingdom of God, even though I wish that all had their human rights.

We need to be sensitive to receive from such movements that which is given by God and to strengthen it, and at the same time we must reject what is not good. But we cannot be complacent. Complacency is the worst sin.

*J. H. Arnold* [3]

THE MOST REMARKABLE thing about the mystery
*149*
of the people of God is that wherever they are, they
perceive the same seed of God and see the same light
gleaming and feel the same warm rays. Wherever human
beings break down under the world's suffering, wherever
hearts feel their own poverty and long for the Spirit,
wherever the ardent revolutionary desire for social justice
arises, wherever the passionate protest against war and
bloodshed rings out, wherever people are persecuted
because of their pacifism or their feeling for social justice,
wherever purity of heart and genuine compassion are to be
found—there they hear his footsteps in history, there they
see the approach of his kingdom, there they anticipate the
blissfulness to come.

*E. Arnold* [4]

*150*   PAUL SAYS THAT Christians are the ambassadors of the coming kingdom. An embassy lives according to the laws of its own kingdom, not according to the laws of the kingdom that surrounds it. This is why the Church of Jesus Christ does not live by the laws of the world around it. The Church lives by the law of the Spirit, whereas present-day governments and nations and capitalistic enterprises do not live by the law of the Spirit. They do not live according to the Spirit of God's future, but according to the requirements of the immediate present. But Christ wants to keep us free of all this for ever and ever. This is the fight into which the church is placed.

*E. Arnold* [5]

OUR LONGING is for a kingdom of peace and
nonviolence, a kingdom of freedom rooted in God. The
critique and rejection of the prevailing conditions
demands a positive counter-move from us, as an example.
All the more just because we criticized capitalism, class
hatred, murder, war, and deceit in social relationships, we
were forced to dare a new, completely different life in a
practical sense. We became a community of a few people
from various classes, trades, and professions. It was a
matter of becoming champions of love to men, of refusing
to bear arms, of building community against the demands
of state, church, private property, and all privileges.

*Gertrud Dalgas* [6]

*152*   THE DEVELOPMENT of mankind shows us that the world will never evolve toward redemption. Salvation and redemption will not come from men; they must come from God. The new kingdom cannot be man-made; it must be given from God, and because of this we are urged to call on God that once again he reveal his kingdom of righteousness and justice.

Jesus was proclaimed by the prophets for thousands of years. He was foretold as the Prince of Peace. And then he came, seemingly very insignificant, a little baby in a feeding trough. But when his mission started, every deed was the kingdom of God. He, Jesus, was the kingdom of God. If he personally forgave sins, that then was the kingdom of God; if he gathered his friends in unity, then the kingdom of God was there. He drove out demons and impure spirits—that was the kingdom of God.

When Jesus was crucified he testified that his death would bring the remission of sins for many; God's spirit could come to men, and the door of heaven would be opened. This sacrifice was brought about by Jesus voluntarily to defeat the prince of this world.

*J. H. Arnold* [7]

**THE KINGDOM OF GOD** has come! Listen to the            *153*
good news: "The time is fulfilled, and the kingdom of God
is at hand; repent, and believe in the gospel" (Mk 1:15). Of
course the kingdom of God is to be consummated in the
future at the end of history at a time "which the Father has
fixed by his own authority" (Acts 1:7). But the salvation
that Jesus has brought to the world is not at the end of
history. God purposes his gift of salvation to be in our
history now. Not partial salvation that leaves out salvation
from the curse of violence and war. "We were by nature
children of wrath, like the rest of mankind. But God, who
is rich in mercy . . . made us alive together with Christ . . .
and raised us up with him, and made us sit with him in the
heavenly places in Christ Jesus" (Eph. 2:3–6). He
"delivered us from the dominion of darkness and
transferred us to the kingdom of his beloved Son" (Col.
1:13). The new life in the kingdom of God is the key to the
peace of Jesus.

*H. Goeringer*

*154*    IN EVERY AGE Jesus calls his church to proclaim the
good news that he is present in the Holy Spirit to bring the
reign of God to our hearts and minds *now* and enable us to
live in his peaceable kingdom right where we are. Since
Jesus died and rose again we are confronted with a life and
death decision—the decision whether Jesus' self-emptying
love revealed on the cross is to rule in the kingdom of God
within us, or whether self-seeking sin is to rule our heart as
we continue to live in the kingdom of a fallen world. It is
the most radical of decisions. It is either/or, not both/and.
It's either the kingdom of God and peace, or the kingdom
of the world and violence.

*H. Goeringer*

JESUS SAID, "Seek first the kingdom of God and his righteousness, and everything else will be yours as well." If we really burn for the kingdom of God first of all, everything else will also be given.

Now it is quite clearly not the kingdom of God if bombs are dropped on innocent people. It is not the kingdom of God if there is racial hatred among men, or if there is such a poor distribution of food that some nations starve while others have surplus food. It is also not the kingdom of God if more and more people are replaced by automation and cannot find work. If we really feel the injustice of this world and long for the kingdom of God, then its righteousness will break in. It will come when the hearts of men are moved toward love and peace.

*J. H. Arnold* [8]

*156*   THE DAWN of the new time lights up the invisible city of peace. The hidden land of fellowship rises into view. In the Holy Spirit of the church, the new Jerusalem comes down. It is the city of perfection, the city without a temple; it has done away with everything cultic. Its life of fellowship *is* the great King's temple of peace.

*E. Arnold* [9]


THE CHURCH BEARS the sevenfold light of the sabbath of peace, when man's own work shall rest for ever because God's great work has begun in quiet. The city of peace and joy opens up the brilliance of the new creation. The first things have passed. The last enter with power. Everything becomes new.

*E. Arnold* [10]


THE PRESENT WORLD can see an image of the city of peace in the church community . This image is a signpost to the future. All must see it. Not one corner of the earth can be left in the dark.

*E. Arnold* [11]

**THE JUSTICE OF JESUS CHRIST** is better than  *157*
that of all moralists and theologians, better than that of all
socialists, communists, and pacifists. For in it flows the sap
of the living plantation of total future peace. Here the
strength of salt, God's innermost essence, is at work. Here
the light from God's heart shines out as the beacon fire of
the city on the hill whose towers proclaim freedom, unity,
and surrender. Here each one wills and does for all
whatever he desires for himself. Here no one gathers a
fortune of his own. Here no heart grows cold in icy fear
and worry about his own economic survival. Here rules the
peace of love.

*E. Arnold* [12]

**ALL CITIZENS OF** God's kingdom are unswervingly
concentrated on the one goal—God's will and God's rule,
God's heart and God's being. Here no one stands opposed
to another. No one is condemned. Nothing is forced upon
anyone. No one is despised. No one is violated. Love reigns
as truth.

*E. Arnold* [13]

*158*  A LIVING FELLOWSHIP of hearts, in a firmly welded bond of all working forces and material goods, stands out in thorough contrast to the conduct of the whole world. This necessarily causes particular bitterness in quarters where people are being recruited for deeds of violence that are justified in ideological terms. For in such a fellowship, every hostile action is rejected outright, no matter what weighty justification is found for it. All participation in warlike, political, or juridical proceedings is excluded, no matter how plausibly it is justified on the grounds of protecting the good. Nor can one have anything to do with violent uprisings, even though they seem necessary in the name of oppressed justice. The very existence and nature of this symbolic life provokes and combats all, right or left, who think that government by force is the highest duty of the hour.

*E. Arnold* [14]

**LOVE FORGOES** everything of its own. Anyone who by     *159*
a clear conscience protects the mystery of his faith will stay
away from any dealings with legal or hostile actions, just as
the elders of the early church did. The justice of Christ will
not sue. It does not act as intermediary. It does no business
to the disadvantage of its neighbor. It abandons all
advantage, sacrifices every privilege, and never defends its
rights. This justice will not sit on any jury, take away
anyone's freedom, or pass a death sentence. It knows no
enemies and will not fight anyone. It will not go to war
against any nation or kill any human being.

*E. Arnold* [15]

*160*     *"This is the hour of victory for our God, the hour of his salvation
and power, when his Christ comes to his rightful rule!"*
(Rev. 12:10)

LORD OUR GOD, in praise and thanksgiving we look
toward your kingdom and the reign of Jesus Christ in your
kingdom. We rejoice that you make him Lord not only in
heaven but also on earth, where he will gain the victory in
all mankind. Men will become good and will love one
another, and they will find peace when everything is done
according to your will. For the time must come when, on
earth as in heaven, your will is done everywhere and in
everything. Be with us with your Spirit so that we may stand
firm as your children until the moment comes for us to
exult: Up out of all grief and trouble! Up from evil and
death! Up to you, our Father in heaven! Praise to your
name today while we are still groaning. Glory to your
kingdom. Glory to Jesus Christ our Savior, whom you have
given us. Amen.

*C. F. Blumhardt* [16]

# ENDNOTES

## CHRISTIAN NONVIOLENCE

[1] *Lift Thine Eyes,* October 19.
[2] *Salt and Light,* 61–62.
[3] *God's Revolution,* 179–180.
[4] EA 11.
[5] EA 27/3.
[6] EA 32/11.
[7] *Inner Land,* 248.
[8] *Salt and Light,* 60.
[9] Ibid., 62–63.

## PEACE IN THE OLD TESTAMENT

[1] *Lift Thine Eyes,* June 11.

## MAN'S NEED FOR REDEMPTION

[1] *Lift Thine Eyes,* July 28.
[2] December 31, 1972.
[3] 1939.
[4] *Salt and Light,* 60.
[5] *Eberhard Arnold: A Testimony,* 49–50.
[6] December 31, 1963.
[7] *Eberhard Arnold: A Testimony,* 48–49.
[8] March 31, 1974.
[9] *Eberhard Arnold: A Testimony,* 49.

*162*  BE SUBJECT TO
GOVERNING AUTHORITIES

[1] *Lift Thine Eyes,* June 8.
[2] Theophilus of Antioch, I,11.
[3] *The Early Christians,* 234–235.
[4] Ibid., 22.
[5] *The Chronicle,* 285.
[6] *The Early Christians,* 19.
[7] Ibid., 108.
[8] *The Chronicle,* 236.
[9] EA 263.
[10] Ibid.
[11] *The Chronicle,* 443.
[12] *The Early Christians,* 97.
[13] *The Chronicle,* 139.
[14] *Salt and Light,* 65.
[15] *The Early Christians,* 303.
[16] *The Chronicle,* 404.
[17] EA 263.

OUR VIOLENT CULTURE

[1] *Lift Thine Eyes,* November 11.
[2] EA 23/11.
[3] April 12, 1968.
[4] *Songs of Light,* #130.

DISCIPLESHIP

[1] *Lift Thine Eyes,* May 1.
[2] *Salt and Light,* 162.

[3] Ibid., 24–25.
[4] *The Early Christians*, 120.
[5] *Salt and Light*, 24.
[6] EA 21/02.
[7] *Salt andLight*, 169–170.
[8] Ibid., 171.
[9] Ibid., 168.
[10] EA 337 in PP 81/1.
[11] *Salt and Light*, 65–66.
[12] Ibid., 64.
[13] Ibid., 63–64.
[14] December 13, 1964.
[15] EA 33/33.
[16] *Songs of Light*, #132.
[17] *Salt and Light*, 54.

## LOVE YOUR ENEMY

[1] *Lift Thine Eyes*, July 27.
[2] *Salt and Light*, 163.
[3] Ibid., 163.
[4] Ibid., 56–57.

## MARTYRDOM

[1] *Lift Thine Eyes*, April 24.
[2] *Salt and Light*, 57.
[3] Ibid., 161.
[4] *The Early Christians*, 155–156.
[5] EA 35/41.
[6] *The Plough*, #4.

The Kingdom of God

[1] *Lift Thine Eyes,* June 10.
[2] EA 23/11.
[3] January 3, 1965.
[4] *Salt and Light,* 28–29.
[5] EA 337 in PP 81/1.
[6] quoted in EA 29/5.
[7] December 13, 1964.
[8] February 14, 1965.
[9] *Salt and Light,* 171.
[10] Ibid., 171–172.
[11] Ibid., 172.
[12] Ibid., 163–164.
[13] Ibid., 164.
[14] Ibid., 165.
[15] Ibid., 167.
[16] *Lift Thine Eyes,* March 20.

# About the Authors

## Howard Goeringer

Howard Goeringer graduated from Union Theological Seminary in 1939. Over the years he has served several different congregations and worked in all of them to bring down walls of racial segregation. He has also been active in a ministry to drug addicts in Newark, New Jersey.

In 1971 Howard and his wife Marge moved to central Florida, where he worked with low-income migrant farm workers in a self-help housing program. Since 1977 they have lived in Tallahassee. Howard has served as minister to a growing Haitian community, as a member of Good News Ministries, as the founder of Agape House, and as editor of *The Jesus Journal*.

Married for almost sixty years, Howard and Marge have five daughters, all married: two are social workers, two are nurses, and one is a teacher. They are blessed with thirteen grandchildren.

*166* EBERHARD ARNOLD (*1883–1935*)

Though little known today, Eberhard Arnold was widely sought-after during his lifetime as a public speaker, writer, lecturer, and publisher in his native Germany. During and after his studies at Breslau, Halle, and Erlangen (from which he received his doctorate in 1909) he was active in the student revival movement then sweeping those cities and became secretary of the German Christian Student Union. In 1916 he became literary director of the Furche Publishing House in Berlin and editor of its monthly.

Like thousands of young Germans in the 1920s, Eberhard and his wife Emmy were disillusioned by the failure of the establishment—especially the churches—to provide answers for the problems of society in the turbulent years following World War I. In their seeking, the Arnolds were influenced by the German Youth Movement (in which Eberhard was a nationally-known particpant), the sixteenth-century Anabaptists, the German pastor Johann Christoph Blumhardt and his son Christoph Friedrich, and most significantly, the early Christians.

In 1920, out of a burning desire to practice the clear demands in the Sermon on the Mount, the Arnolds with their five children and a few others began a communal life in the Hessian village of Sannerz. The community, which supported itself by agriculture and a small but vibrant publishing house, attracted thousands of visitors and grew

quickly. By 1926 the house in Sannerz had become too            *167*
small, and the next year a new *Bruderhof* ("place of
brothers") was started in the nearby Rhön hills.

In 1930 Eberhard went to America, where he spent a
year among the Hutterian Brethren, an Anabaptist group
who had been living in total community since 1528. The
young German Bruderhof was incorporated into the
Hutterian Brethren, and Eberhard was ordained as a
Hutterian servant of the Word (or minister) and
missionary in Germany. Eberhard died in Darmstadt as the
result of complications following an amputation.

1933 and the years following brought the Bruderhof
persecution by the National Socialist regime and expulsion
from Germany. After a temporary stay in neighboring
Liechtenstein, the group fled to England. World War II
drove the Bruderhof to Paraguay, and in the 1950s new
communities in New York, Connecticut, and Pennsylvania
were established.

Today, in 1994, there are Bruderhofs in Canada, the
United States, England, Germany, Nigeria, and Japan.

## *168* CHRISTOPH FRIEDRICH BLUMHARDT *(1842–1919)*

The son of the south-German pastor Johann Christoph Blumhardt, C. F. Blumhardt is widely known in Germany and Switzerland as the founder of religious socialism in Europe.

"Jesus is victor!" the motto of the elder Blumhardt, became the foundation of his son's ministry, and on it he built a radical Christianity that proclaimed, "Die to yourselves, and Jesus will live! God's kingdom is coming!"

Though known as a pastor and writer rather than a theologian, C. F. Blumhardt (and his father) deeply influenced the most important thinkers of their day, including Karl Barth, Paul Tillich, Emil Brunner, and Dietrich Bonhoeffer. At the Bruderhof, writings of the Blumhardts have been especially valued for their witness to the reality of God and his intervening power—not only in world history, but in the personal lives of every man and woman.

# BIBLIOGRAPHY

Arnold, Eberhard, ed. *The Early Christians after the Death of*    *169*
the Apostles. Rifton, NY: Plough, 1972.

————. *Inner Land: A Guide into the Heart and Soul of the
Bible.* Rifton, NY: Plough, 1976.

————. *Salt and Light: Talks and Writings on the Sermon on the
Mount.* Rifton, NY: Plough, 1967.

Blumhardt, Christoph. *Lift Thine Eyes: Evening Prayers.*
Rifton, NY: Plough, 1988.

Ewert, J. Georg. "Christ or Country?" *The Plough* 4 (May
1984): 6–10.

Hutterian Brethren, ed. and trans. *The Chronicle of the
Hutterian Brethren, Volume I.* Rifton, NY: Plough, 1987.

Hutterian Society of Brothers, ed. *Eberhard Arnold: A
Testimony of Church Community from his Life and Writings.*
Rifton, NY: Plough, 1973.

Hutterian Society of Brothers, ed. *Songs of Light: The
Bruderhof Songbook.* Rifton, NY: Plough, 1977.

*170*    Hutterian Brethren and Yoder, John Howard, ed. *God's Revolution: The Witness of Eberhard Arnold.* New York: Paulist Press, 1984, reprint Plough, 1992

**A complete listing of books from Plough is available on request. Write to:**

Plough Publishing House
Spring Valley Bruderhof
Rd 2 Box 446  Rt 381 N
Farmington PA 15437-9506
Tel. (412) 329–1100